Empath

Survival Guide for Empaths, Become a Healer Instead

of Absorbing Negative Energies.

A Complete Guide for Developing Your Gift and Overcoming Fears

Contents

Chapter 19 – Emotional Intelligence and Self-Awareness

Conclusion

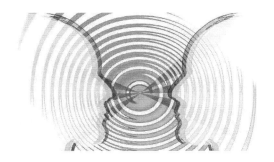

Introduction

This book contains key information, lessons, and strategies that will let you effectively apply empathy and emotional intelligence on the way you interact, relate, and understand the people around you.

Over the years, researchers have recognized the importance of empathy and, in a broader sense, emotional intelligence. There has been much debate on how to define it, how to apply it in everyday situations, and most important, how someone can develop their empathic and other emotional skills. You can find out the answers to this question and more by carefully absorbing the contents of this book, and assessing yourself to determine if you are indeed an empathic and emotionally intelligent person.

Sub-divided into nineteen chapters, this book covers the following topics:

- What is an Empath?

    In this chapter, you will learn what an empath is, and its five subtypes. Discussed here as well are the factors that differentiate empathy from sympathy and compassion.

- What Does It Mean to Be an Empath?

  To better explain what it means to be an empath, this chapter goes over the benefits and challenges faced by individuals gifted with this special ability.

- What are the Signs of an Empath?

  Discover the 38 signs to look out for in order to tell if you are exhibiting traits and abilities expected from an empath.

- Are Empaths Born or Developed?

  Presented in this chapter are the different theories and arguments about the true nature and origins of an empath.

- How to Know If You're an Empath

  A quick way to check if you are an empath is by doing a self-assessment. This chapter contains a 25-item test that will shed light on your ability as an empath.

- The Differences Between Sensitive People and Empaths

  Find out if a sensitive person and an empath are synonymous by comparing their qualities and capabilities.

- Everything You Need to Know About Empath's Personality Type

  Learn which of the five personality types an empath can fall under.

- The Main Empath Traits

  Discover the seven main traits exhibited by all empaths.

- How to Develop Your Gifts and Talents

  Empathy can be learned and developed by following the tips and strategies given in this chapter.

- How Negative Energy Directly Impacts on an Empath

  Discussed in this chapter are the various ways negative energy affects the lives of empaths.

- How to Protect Yourself from Energy Vampires

  Learn the strategies and techniques that empaths can employ to mitigate the negative effects being around energy vampires.

- Methods to Fight Negative Energy

  Equip yourself with 12 effective strategies to combat negative energy.

- Emotional Intelligence

  Discover what emotional intelligence is and its five components.

- The Power of Emotional Intelligence

  Learn the value and power of emotionally intelligent leaders and employees in the workplace.

- Managing Your Emotions

  Find out how to effectively deal with your negative emotions.

- Understanding Others

  Learn how to improve your capacity to understand the people around you.

- Managing Your Relationship

  Improve both your intimate and social relationships with the power of emotional intelligence.

- Emotional Intelligence and Health

  Discover the effects of emotional intelligence on your physical and mental health.

- Emotional Intelligence and Self-Awareness

Find out how you can properly recognize and acknowledge your own emotions.

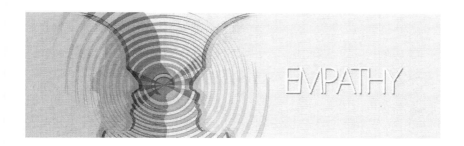

Chapter 1 – What is an Empath?

An empath is someone who possesses a high level of awareness of the emotions felt by other people. Individuals with this ability can experience both positive and negative feelings of others as if they were his or she own. Many experts believe that having this gift makes someone more emotionally and socially intelligent than the average person. As such, numerous studies have been conducted in order to fully define and understand the characteristics and abilities of an empath.

Empathy vs. Sympathy vs. Compassion

Before delving into the complexities of being an empath, it is important to understand first the distinctions among the concepts of sympathy, compassion, and empathy. Some people use these terms interchangeably. However, once examined in detail, many would realize how empaths differ from people who sympathize or feel compassionate over the plight of others.

At the most basic level, sympathy and compassion refer to one's personal feelings towards another individual. When one sees another person suffering, it is normal to feel bad for the person who is actually experiencing pain or despair. One component that separates one from the other is the element of action attributed to compassion.

Nowadays, sympathizing with another person has taken on a more passive tone. This is why greeting card companies have a separate category for sympathy-themed cards. Expressing commiseration or feeling pity for a person who has a stroke of bad luck shows that you are sympathizing with them. Feeling compelled to do something about that person's unfortunate situation indicates a certain level of compassion towards others. Neither of these two, however, means that you are feeling that person's pain and suffering on a personal level.

Through the immense power of the mind, empaths are able to connect with the emotions of others, ranging from inexplicable joy to absolute misery. Like other skills, empathy can be honed through regular practice and going through personal experiences. Without this level of dedication, empaths are naturally vulnerable to the downsides of being exposed to the stress and negative energy of other people. Fortunately, aiming for the complete mastery of empathic abilities is not an impossible feat to achieve.

The Five Types of Empaths

According to experts, empaths can be categorized into five subsets: cognitive empaths, emotional empaths, compassionate empaths, somatic empaths, and spiritual empaths. All five types possess the common traits associated with empathy. However, points of divergence rise based on how the empath handles the emotions that he or she is sensing from others.

- Cognitive Empaths

  Cognitive empaths process the thoughts and feelings of others in a logical and rational manner rather than in an emotional way like the other types do. Because of this, some researchers in the field of interest refer to this as "perspective-oriented empathy" or "empathy by thought."

  Having this ability is useful when you have to engage with others in a professional setting, such as interviews and negotiations. The cognitive empath would be able to himself or herself into the shoes of the other person without having to deal with the more emotional aspects of their encounter. Though this does not fit completely with the basic definition of empathy that most people know, cognitive empathy is considered by experts as a sub-category mainly due to its perceptive and sensitive nature.

  A rather dark but illustrative example of this ability in action is those who employ torture as an interrogation technique. Using cognitive empathy, the torturers would be able to devise more effective ways of hurting someone to get information without having to feel pity or sympathy.

- Emotional empaths

  These empaths possess the qualities that more commonly associated with the concept of empathy. According to research studies, it is also most likely the first brush with empathy that everyone experiences during early childhood. It can be observed among babies who smile back to their parents whenever they see them smiling at them. Similarly, some experts believe that this ability is at play too when babies cry after hearing the sound of other children or babies crying.

  Being an emotional empath is reportedly beneficial among those in the service and care industries. For example, nurses would be able to better attend to the needs of their patients if they could understand and feel their emotions as if they were their own. They would be able to sense distress and pain, even when the patient is unable to express their feelings due to their condition.

  On the other hand, people with emotional empathy are vulnerable towards the so-called "empathy overload", which would then lead them to be burnt out emotionally. As such, they need to learn techniques on how better regulate their personal emotions and control their reactions towards whatever stimuli is affecting them.

- Compassionate Empaths

  Compassionate empaths feel the urge to help others whenever they sense the distress and other negative emotions of those around them. This is consistent with the concept of pure compassion, wherein the person feels concern about someone else, and therefore feels the need to act on eliminating the problem or mitigating its effects. The main difference lies in the level of understanding that empaths and compassionate have towards other people.

  Many experts believe that this is the ideal form of empathy. In general, people would appreciate your ability to understand their situation, but only to a certain extent. Bursting out in tears would also not be of much value towards those in need, no matter how deeply you feel for their plights. Without extending out a helping hand, they might feel like that, you are merely expressing your sympathies or even pity towards them. The initiative to assist others in their time of need is what sets apart compassionate empaths from the other types of empaths, thus giving them a more favorable reputation among experts in this field.

- Somatic Empaths

  One of the lesser recognized types of empaths; somatic empaths primarily feel the physical pain of other people, rather than emotions and thoughts. For example, witnessing someone being punched hard on the face would make the somatic empath feel a similar smacking sensation on his or her face.

  Most cases of somatic empaths are observed among identical twins. Furthermore, in rare cases wherein the twins were separated at birth, at least one of the twins would report experiencing an inexplicable physical trauma. It would usually turn out that the other twin had actually experienced the incident that caused the trauma at around the same time.

  Researchers suggest that this is proof of how somatic empathy works. The echoes of physical sensations, particularly pain, travels and hits those who are vulnerable and receptive to them.

- Spiritual Empaths

  This is the least studied of all the types of empaths, mainly because it bears more similarities with Eastern traditional philosophies rather than modern neuroscience and psychology. Still, this is considered as one of the primary types of empath due to its nature and general qualities.

  Unlike other types of empaths, spiritual empaths are said to possess stronger and closer connections with a higher consciousness or otherworldly beings. They are more sensitive and receptive towards the energy and messages from other dimensions, thus giving them more special psychic abilities.

  Some experts compare this to the concept of personal enlightenment that many Eastern religions strive for. Thus, it is said that spiritual empaths can hone their skills through regular and proper meditation.

Take note that the different types of empaths are not mutually exclusive from one another. This means that someone who exhibits signs of being a somatic empath can also be an emotional empath at the same time. Being categorized into one label, however, suggests that the empath is primarily showing qualities that are more associated with that particular type.

Much like anything that is distributed along a spectrum, finding the right balance is the key to making the most out of one's empathic abilities. Simply feeling and understanding others does not make one a good empath. Logic and emotions should always be blended well in order to best utilize one's gifts and potentials. Thus, empaths would benefit from, first, learning what it truly means to be an empath, and, second, experimenting with the many ways one can grow as a full-fledged empath.

Chapter 2 – What Does It Mean to Be an Empath?

One way of understanding empaths is to consider the benefits and challenges of having this special gift. Due to their sensitive and receptive nature, both the highs and lows of possessing this ability can significantly affect all aspects of the empath's life. As such, there has been a lot of discussion of whether empathy is actually a blessing or a curse.

Benefits of Being an Empath

People who do not understand empathy think that it is some sort of superpower, like telepathy or clairvoyance. This assumption is most likely rooted in the reported benefits of having this ability. However, when studied closer, empathy is nothing like those unproven parapsychological skills. To better explain this point, here are the main benefits of being an empath. Examine how close these are to your own experiences because, as some researchers suggest, all humans are born empathic—though the level of this ability varies from one person to another depending on certain factors.

- Feel and Understand the Emotions of Other People

  This is one of the hallmark traits of empathy, and it has a wide range of uses. For instance, an empath can sense if their friend or colleague is feeling anxious. By being sensitive enough to notice this, he or she would be able to provide appropriate support to those in need.

- Higher Capacity for Love and Compassion

  Empaths experience positive emotions on a greater scale. This is particularly evident when an empath is in a relationship. Communicating one's feelings to his or her partner could be a tough feat to achieve. Empaths, on the other hand, are natural at this for they can recognize their partners' true emotions even without hearing the words from them. Because of their high awareness of how others feel, they are able to use love and compassion as foundations of their relationships.

- Proclivity for Creative Expressions

  Since they feel emotions intensely, empaths seek ways to express themselves through creative means. They channel their feelings and unique energy into different forms of art, which can move and connect with other people. Engaging themselves in creative activities also allow them to revitalize both their bodies and minds.

- Effectively Read Non-Verbal Cues

  Aside from recognizing the feelings of other people, empaths are also sensitive towards non-verbal cues that give away the real thoughts and feelings of those around them. A person might be saying that they are completely fine, but their facial expressions and tone of the voice say otherwise. Empaths are natural at learning how to read these cues and figure out the meaning behind one's words.

Challenges of Being an Empath

Experts agree that the best way to handle the challenges faced by empaths is to develop coping mechanisms and strategies to regulate or even eliminate the troublesome issues associated with this gift. Doing so would allow empaths to better utilize their special abilities and enjoy more the benefits of possessing an empathic mind.

The first step to achieve that state of understanding the challenges that empaths face. Here is a list of the most common personal issues according to people who are gifted with empathy:

- Overstimulation

  Due to the lowered defenses against stimuli, many empaths feel as if their nerve endings are being rubbed raw whenever exposed to an increased level of sensory information. The threshold for the acceptable level of stimuli is much lower, thereby leading to the appearance of more symptoms of being burned out.

Some empaths can handle this issue on their own by simply seeking space and time where they could be very alone. Those who cannot do so tend to suffer in silence from the negative effects of overstimulation.

- Absorption of Other People's Stress and Negativity

Many empaths report having moments of confusion over whether the stress and negativity they are feeling belong to them or if they are merely receiving the negative vibes that other people are giving off. For them, there would always be a chance that the bodily discomfort or mental stress they are suffering from does not originate within themselves, but rather from the people around them.

When not addressed properly, this issue can elevate from a minor disturbance in your system to a full breakdown of your body and mind. As attested by many research studies, increased levels of stress lead to the development of physical and mental complications, such as constant feelings of fatigue, pain, and anxiety.

- Extremely Intense Feelings

  Empaths naturally feel things more intensely compared to regular people. A sad story might be able to draw out a frown or momentary unhappiness from non-empaths. The same story, on the other hand, can elicit sorrow, frustration, or anger from empaths since they can feel things as if they had personally gone through the sad events of the story.

  This tendency to feel things more intensely becomes a bigger problem when an empath is exposed to upsetting or violent media. People with this ability could not only be a mere viewer of the events unfolding before them. Without the ability to regulate their empathic nature, they are going to feel agony and despair as intensely as the persons who are actually suffering.

- Emotional and Social Hangovers

  Due to sensory overload, empaths are vulnerable to experiencing the emotions of others after being exposed to those emotions for an extended period. The duration of these so-called hangovers varies from one empath to another, but the symptoms include physical fatigue, headaches, and lingering feelings of anxiety, depending on the kind of energy and vibes that they have absorbed from others.

- Feelings of Isolation and Loneliness

Some empaths who have not learned how to properly handle their special gifts opt to stay away from other people instead of facing their condition head-on. As such, those who do not know or understand their reasons for doing so may begin to view the empaths as cold and standoffish.

There are also empaths who become overly aware of their surroundings, making them seem paranoid to others. They may find themselves inadvertently freezing when in the presence of others, leading the people around to believe that such behaviors stem from social ineptitude. Without the proper mindset and defense mechanisms, empaths run the risk of caging themselves away from other people just to avoid the other downsides of possessing their special abilities.

- Emotional Burnout

The thing with being a good and compassionate listener is that it draws more people towards you. Empaths are naturally good at understanding one's side of the story. All types of empaths are good at doling out pieces of advice, and some are even compelled to act on their own advice to aid those in need.

The problem begins when the empaths overextend themselves. It is admirable to feel compassion towards the unfortunate situations of other people. However, self-care is important as well. Failing to draw the line and set boundaries would inevitably cause the empath to suffer from emotional burnout.

- Increased Sensitivity to Various Environmental Stimuli

Many empaths cannot stand bright lights, strong smells, spicy food, extreme temperatures, and loud noises. A large number of stimuli from their surroundings overwhelm their already sensitive bodies and minds. At worst, these intense sensory experiences could turn into full-blown panic attacks, especially when an empath is not equipped to handle such situations.

- Heightened Need for Space and Boundaries in Intimate Relationships

When it comes to living together or sharing a bed with their intimate partners, some empaths require special arrangements in order to keep themselves comfortable. Communication between the empath and their loved ones is key to effectively handling this.

Unfortunately, some empaths might feel like they are being selfish with their requests and boundaries. That kind of thinking, if not addressed, could lead to dissatisfaction, loneliness and other problems within the relationship.

Figuring out what it means to be an empath requires you to gain a holistic insight on both their good and bad experiences. With this level of understanding, you will be able to ground your expectations on what empaths could do, and what limitations are imposed upon them by the nature of this special ability.

Chapter 3 – What are the Signs of an Empath?

Empaths are gifted with the special ability to understand a person's feelings on a much deeper and personal level. Though considered as a rare talent, empaths are said to make up around fifteen percent of the world's population. Therefore, there is a chance that you are an empath yourself.

To tell if you are one of them, here are 38 signs that you should look out for in your day-to-day living. Remember, either this skill can be naturally present upon birth, or it can also be acquired through observation and personal experiences. This means that you could have been experiencing these signs since you were a child, or you could have just noticed them happening to you recently.

1. You are an effective listener and/or speaker.

   People with high levels of empathy have the ability to make others feel like they are being heard and understood. This is further enhanced by their natural talent of directing conversations so that even the most reserved individuals would be interested in contributing to whatever the topic is.

2. You seem to have a strong intuition.

   Empaths are attuned with their inner selves, thereby giving them a good sense of what is right and proper. They typically use their intuition to read the emotions of other people and figure out the true meanings behind one's words and sentiments.

3. Others describe you as a curious individual or a seeker of truths.

   The unexplainable and unknown—such as paranormal activities and extraterrestrial life—catch the attention of empaths since they have this need to understand life itself. Their intense need for the truth can border on obsessive sometimes, and they tend to pursue their leads until they have uncovered everything there is to know about their current interests.

4. You are strong, but a quiet leader.

   Empaths are not ones to brag about their accomplishments, but they are capable of pushing others into achieving great things. Working behind the scenes, empaths shine as humble yet inspiring leaders.

5. You think outside of the box while still maintaining a clear vision of the future.

Given their creative tendencies, empaths are good at solving problems and pushing boundaries. They do have the ability to remain focused on what they actually want to achieve, thus keeping them focused on what really matters despite the many probable distractions that they might encounter on their way to attaining their goals.

6. People are quick to place their trust onto you.

Strangers are drawn to you, and new acquaintances might even feel like you have known each other for many years despite the lack of actual history between the two of you. Because of your seemingly magnetic pull, other people feel comfortable enough to share with you their personal experiences and opinions.

7. Your interests include healing and holistic wellness.

Empaths are usually interested in pursuing careers that would allow them to take care of those in need. Their typical career paths include being a doctor, nurse, therapist, psychiatrist, homeopath, social worker, or even a veterinarian.

8. You are in touch with your spirituality.

   Spirituality is a concept that captures the interest of empaths. This does not necessarily equate with religion though many empaths find themselves joining religious organizations in order to fulfill their need to belong. Meditation, chakra healing, and other types of spiritual activities are also areas of interests of empaths.

9. You have experienced lucid dreaming.

   Vivid dreams are usually experienced by empaths even at a young age. Over time, this could escalate further into lucid dreaming, wherein the person is able to remain somewhat in control while in the state of dreaming. After such episodes, empaths are usually able to describe in incredible detail their dreams, and some could even develop a desire to interpret the meanings behind their dreams.

10. You enjoy expressing your creativity in various ways.

    Empaths express their creativity through painting, dancing, acting, designing, singing, or playing a musical instrument. Their stories captivate their audience since their ability to feel the emotions of other people can translate to having a vivid imagination.

11. You frequently find yourself daydreaming whenever you feel bored.

    If whatever they are doing, fails to sufficiently stimulating them, empaths usually resort to daydreaming in order to keep themselves occupied or entertained. This tendency could also manifest in other forms, such as doodling on a piece of paper, humming a tune, or fidgeting with whatever object they are holding at that given moment.

12. You want to learn more about ancient civilizations and/or indigenous cultures.

    Traditions and long-held beliefs tend to hold the interests of empaths, but not out of simple curiosity or preference for the logical or practical ways of doing things. Empaths tend to challenge societal norms and expectations, even when something has been already tested by time.

13. Your ancestral lineage interests you.

    Even as young children, empaths enjoy listening to family stories that are passed on to the next generation. They are genuinely interested in learning their origins, and who their ancestors were. According to experts, this interest likely stems from the empaths' need to connect with other people without being hurt or burdened by their emotions and negative energies.

14. Antiques or vintage items draw your attention.

Even by simply holding objects with a long history behind it, empaths are able to read the energy emanating from them and discover some important facts about its previous owners. However, if an empath is still inexperienced, this could be regarded as off-putting to their senses instead. As an empath gains better control of his or her abilities, an appreciation for such items would also begin to develop.

15. You have a natural affinity towards animals and plants.

Typically raised with a pet in their homes, empaths love animals, and as a result, promotes causes that promote the welfare of and prevent cruelty to animals. They also enjoy spending time in nature, surrounded by plants and beautiful landscapes. Being in such surroundings allow them to regenerate their energy and restore their focus.

16. You actively seek for adventures and opportunities to be spontaneous.

Empaths enjoy traveling to new places or doing activities that they have never done before. Free-spirited by nature, they would sometimes get the impulse to leave everything behind and explore the world. Otherwise, empaths could grow restless from being stagnant in one place for a significant period of time.

17. You exhibit great appreciation and enthusiasm for life.

    One of the life goals of many empaths is to live life at its fullest. This requires them to expend so much energy that suffering from a burnout becomes a normal thing for them. They also do not do things half-heartedly, so they get disappointed when the people around them do not share the same zest for life.

18. At heart, you are a humanitarian who aspires for peace and harmony.

    Regardless if it is between their family, friends, colleagues, or even strangers, empaths are extremely unsettled whenever they are in conflict with others. That is why they immediately try to find ways to resolve the situation or to reach a compromise that would work for everyone involved.

19. You are giver, not a receiver.

    Empaths tend to give everything they have without expecting anything in return. Sometimes, they overdo this, leaving them drained or lonely. Those around them might fail to realize this, so empaths usually look inwards for ways to restore themselves. When all else fails, they might be forced to bottle up their frustrations instead, which would then lead to worse problems later on.

20. You nurture others without enabling their unhealthy tendencies.

Though they have a deep understanding of how the other person feels, empaths are not going to tell someone what they want to hear just for the sake of appeasing them. They always side with the truth, and when combined with their helpful nature, they would rather point out a person's wrongdoings than gloss over the fact mistakes have been committed by the said person.

21. You enjoy doing water-related activities.

Swimming in the sea, spending time at the pool, soaking in a hot tub—empaths feel calm and relaxed whenever they are near a body or source of water. Healing is normally associated with water, so they relish spending time in it.

22. You need to have alone time.

Even though empaths are naturally social beings, they always seek for opportunities to escape from their day-to-day responsibilities and interactions with other people. This could be simple respites, such as reading a book alone or taking a nap or this could extend to taking long vacations on their own.

23. Public places easily overwhelm you.

Whenever you go to a supermarket, stadiums, or other places where a crowd can gather, a wave of anxiety and panic takes over you. This usually happens because you are vulnerable towards the myriad of emotions around you, regardless of whether or not an emotion is directed at you.

24. Your mood swings are unpredictable.

Empaths feel the highs and lows of a moment in an intense manner. Depending on the situation they are in, they could be ecstatic for one minute and then depressed on the next. This is not usually just their own emotions, but also rather a product of emotions that they have picked up from others.

25. You are strongly affected by violent or cruel scenes in a movie, TV show, or in real life.

Though they are just witnessing the scene, empaths tend to be strongly affected by scenes of extreme violence, abuse, or pain. In some cases, they may even feel physically ill over the mere sight of violence or cruelty. They also have a hard time processing why those kinds of acts happen to other people.

26. You are averse towards fighting with someone for any reason.

Whether it is a physical or verbal fight, empaths are not ones to engage others in a fight. If the other person is not willing to let the issue go, they are quick to feel frustrated or annoyed about the situation, not usually the other person.

27. You tend to back down during confrontations.

Since they understand, sometimes to a fault, empaths feel like they should give way to others rather than stand up for themselves. They also have a hard time expressing negative emotions towards others since they know the impact it could have on them.

28. Breakups are extremely hard for you.

Empaths cannot burn bridges, even when they have a toxic relationship with someone. They are unable to walk away easily since they are highly aware of the pain that this would cause to the other person. Instead, they will try to remain with that person until everything becomes too unbearable for both of them. At that point, hurting the other person becomes inevitable, thus causing extreme misery to the empaths themselves.

29. Forgiveness comes too easily to you.

    Even if the other person does not deserve it, empaths seem to be always ready to forgive. Since they are able to connect with others on a deeper level, these individuals are not likely to hold on to grudges for a long period. They also see things from the perspective of the other person, and this could be a good thing when done in moderation. However, some people try to take advantage of their forgiving nature, which could then lead to unhealthy relationships.

30. You feel the pain, stress, and negative emotions of other people.

    Because of their heightened senses to physical energy and emotions, empaths absorb the negative energies coming off people around them. Their tendency to mirror emotions prevent them from effectively distinguishing their own suffering from those of others. This could be effectively addressed, however, when the empath matures and gains a high-level of self-awareness.

31. You are prone to suffering from diseases and/or illnesses.

Because of their vulnerability towards the emotional energies of those around them, this flaw could manifest into actual suffering for the empaths themselves. If an empath would not be able to protect himself or herself adequately, the frequency of catching an illness or a disease would increase over time.

32. You feel exhausted most of the time.

Beyond physical exhaustion, empaths are also likely to experience mental, emotional, and spiritual fatigue. The combination is overwhelming for an empath, which could then cause them to slip into a state of chronic exhaustion.

33. You do not like being in a cluttered environment.

Because of their high levels of sensitivity towards energy, empaths cannot stand being in an environment that is chaotic or filled with clutter. They are also seeking for balance, so they would not hesitate to organize things or rearrange the furniture in order to restore good energy flow in their surroundings.

34. You have a tendency to quickly form an addiction.

Without learning proper coping techniques, some empaths may be tempted to escape from the burdens and responsibilities that their gifts entail. Their escape could come in various forms including alcoholism, binge eating, and usage of recreational drugs, smoking, or even gambling. Empaths who succumb to such unhealthy addictions are usually looking for ways to numb their pain or drown out the emotions and energies from other people.

35. You try to hold back your reactions over a situation or towards another person.

Experienced empaths recognize the power of words, so instead of giving in to the heat of the moment, they hold themselves back in case they say blurt something out that they can no longer take back. In the event that they must react, empaths take great care in choosing their words. The last thing they want is to inadvertently hurt somebody. However, this comes with a big drawback since the pressure to remain calm and levelheaded could become too much for them. When that happens, empaths could either have a breakdown or lash out against the people close to them.

36. People think that you prefer living inside your own head.

Because they are highly sensitive with whatever is going on with their surroundings, empaths are frequently caught unaware as they think about the things that are happening to them and around them. They have a tendency to overthink, which others might think of as being self-absorbed. In reality, however, they usually become caught up with their own minds and emotions without meaning to do so.

37. You have a strong moral compass.

Empaths are always drawn to the truth of the situation. They believe that everyone should be honest, and if someone fails to do this, they do not only feel extremely hurt over this. They can also become disillusioned about their relationship with that person. Empaths also despise any form of injustice since it runs against their personal code of morality.

38. You tend to break the rules.

Due to their creativity, empaths are not the ones to follow rules, routines, or repetitive actions. They seek ways to express themselves, so when they are told not to do so; they challenge the order of things and figure out a way to be true to their spontaneous and adventurous selves.

If you notice that some of the given points above do not apply to you, worry not for that it is perfectly normal. No two empaths are alike, so some of these signs would surely not fit your personality and experiences. There are also signs that seem to contradict with one another, so it is highly improbable for anyone to exhibit or possess these traits at all times.

What matters is that you possess the key traits that make empath special. If you are not sure about whether or not you truly have them, feel free to seek the opinions of those who care about you. They might be able to recognize parts of your being that you are aware of yourself.

Chapter 4 – Are Empaths Born or Developed?

Much like other human abilities, many researchers are interested in determining whether empathy is genetic or learned. The recent surge in interest on empathy has given rise to numerous theories on how the true origins and nature of empathy itself. Though there is no single theory that fully explains this phenomenon, here are five of the most compelling scientific theories from the experts on neuroscience.

Theory #1: Mirror Neurons

There is a specialized group of brain cells that researchers have identified with compassion. These neurons allow humans to mimic the emotions of other people, thus giving them the name "mirror neurons." Following this discovery, many researchers suggest that empaths possess hypersensitive mirror neurons, thus giving them the ability to feel others' joy, sadness, fear, and pain, among others.

Mirror neurons are said to be activated through external events experienced by the person. For instance, if you see your child hurt, you would feel hurt too. If you are feeling sad, your mirror neurons might be reacting towards some external stimuli that are similar to how you are feeling.

Because of how brain cells work, experts who believe in this theory suggest that empaths are born rather than developed. These mirror neurons are already present during one's birth, thus explaining why some babies seem to empathize with their caretakers and other babies.

Theory #2: Electromagnetic Fields

This theory is rooted in the discovery that both the brain and the heart generate its respective electromagnetic fields. According to its proponents, the electromagnetic fields serve as the conduit between one being to another, allowing the transmission of thoughts and emotions to and from everyone.

People with high levels of empathy are more receptive towards these signals, which then cause them to feel overwhelmed by all the information they are receiving from those around them. They are able to better sense any changes in the electromagnetic field, and how these changes could affect and draw out intense reactions from them.

Similar to the first theory, this explanation suggests that empaths are born with this sensitivity towards electromagnetic fields. They do not, however, discount the possibility that one could increase their sensitivity over time and with the correct technique, thereby suggesting too that empathy is an ability that can be developed.

Theory #3: Emotional Contagions

Studies on the concept of emotional contagions have given valuable insights into how empath works. According to this theory, emotions, like diseases, can be picked up by one person by simply being near the individual who is actually bearing it. For example, a single crying infant can set off the entire ward for newborns. An anxious colleague could cause the rest of the office to feel ill at ease.

This synchronicity of the moods among groups of people has also been observed to be beneficial. Being around positive and motivated people can inspire you to follow suit. Thus, empaths are advised to choose the company they keep whenever possible.

This particular theory does not focus much on the origins of empathy. It does imply that humans are naturally capable of picking up emotional contagions. This means that this scientific theory is leaning more on the argument that empaths are born. It should be noted, however, that it also does not offer any counterargument to the idea that empathy is a skill that can be learned and improved.

Theory #4: Increased Dopamine Sensitivity

Some neuroscientists believe that empaths are more sensitive towards the effects of dopamine, a neurotransmitter that is mainly associated with pleasure. According to their research, empaths who have also been identified as introverts, have lower pleasure thresholds than their extraverted counterparts. This means that introverts achieve an acceptable pleasure through simple activities that would hardly stimulate extraverts. In nonprofessional's term, introverted empaths require less dopamine than extraverts do in order to feel happy.

This theory could possibly explain why most empaths prefer spending time alone and doing activities that they could do on their own or with a small group of people only. Being exposed to large social gatherings tire them out because dopamine is flooding their system.

Neuroscientists who proposed this theory suggest that empathy, much like introversion and extraversion, is a human quality that is present at birth. Everyone is predisposed to possessing certain personality traits, and depending on the environment they grow up in, these traits could either be enhanced or downplayed until it entirely disappears.

Theory #5: Mirror-Touch Synesthesia

Synesthesia is a rare neurological condition wherein the person processes sensory stimuli in at least two different ways. For example, some people see specific colors whenever they hear a particular sound. Bursts of red and pink might appear before them as they listen to pop music. Across history, various synesthetic people have made significant impacts in their respective fields. The list includes Sir Isaac Newton and the musician, Billy Joel.

A group of neuroscientists believes that empathy is similar to, if not the same as, the condition called mirror-touch synesthesia. According to their studies, synesthetic people with this particular condition could feel the emotions and physical sensations of others as such feelings were their own. They typically undergo this if they actually see the person expressing an emotion, or if they have physically touched someone who is feeling something in an intense manner.

Though mirror-touch lacks some other components of empathy, this condition remains a probable explanation of how empathy works. Synesthesia itself could occur either at birth or due to a particular trauma experienced at any age. Therefore, this theory does not provide strong arguments for the idea of one being born as an empath. Furthermore, it does not support the idea that empathy is an ability that can be learned since synesthesia is not something that can be developed or enhanced through practice.

Compared to the given neuroscientific theories, the explanations proposed by human development experts suggest that empathy is a learned ability. According to their case studies, the main contributing factor is the type of parental support that one receives as a child. Genetics play an important role too, but only as an indicator of who would likely be an empath later on. Even if a person were predisposed to become an empath due to the empathic abilities of his or her parents, the kind of upbringing he or she will have would determine the level of empathy of this given person.

For you to better understand the standpoint of these researchers here are effects of two different types of parenting on the development of a person's empathic abilities.

- Abusive or Neglectful Parenting

    According to studies on early childhood development, traumas experienced by a person during this stage can significantly affect the level of sensitivity towards emotions and other forms of stimuli by the time the said person has reached adulthood. Many empaths who seek professional help are observed to be from households wherein one or both of the parents are depressed, alcoholic, or violent.

The lack of care and support wears down the natural defenses of a person. This could then result in the noted vulnerability of empaths to the negative emotions of those around them.

Furthermore, since they were not taught how to effectively manage their own emotions, empaths that fall under this category are more likely to absorb the energies and emotions of other people. In most cases, they are also unable to separate the absorbed energy and emotions from their own.

- Supportive Parenting

Studies show that parents serve as one of the first role models for children, especially those who exhibit empathic traits. Therefore, the words and actions of parents contribute to the healthy development of the special gifts possessed by these children.

The lessons picked up during early childhood would continue to evolve as one grows up. Depending on how supportive the parents are, these learned behaviors could either be amplified or toned down. In the case of empaths who were raised in nurturing households, they are able to develop better coping mechanisms compared to those growing up in less than ideal conditions. Since they can better handle the challenges of being an empath, they are also capable of utilizing their gifts significant and helpful ways that benefit themselves and those around them.

Though there is no definite answer on why and how people become empaths, it is still possible to understand the makings of an empath. Efforts to discover the answer to this question are not futile attempts since every information gained could prove useful to empaths who still need guidance on how to remain healthy and functional despite the difficulties of living in the modern world.

Chapter 5 – How to Know If You are an Empath

Recognizing your special gifts as an empath is one of the first steps that you must take in order to properly manage the benefits and challenges of being one. This would also help you create and maintain good relationships with those around you.

The best person to assess whether or not you are an empath is yourself. Even though empathy involves the energy and emotions of other people, this ability is still primarily centered on your personal thoughts and feelings. Hence, the most effective way of confirming this is through a guided self-assessment.

Self-Assessment Test on Empathy

Answer the following questions with either "yes" if condition stated describes you or "no" if you have never felt or thought that way. Keep a tally of your responses so that you can ascertain later on your level of empathy.

1. Have you ever been labeled as "shy", "introverted," or "highly sensitive"?

2. Do you often feel worried or overwhelmed?

3. Do you feel uncomfortable whenever you hear someone yelling, even if it is not aimed at you?

4. Do arguments make you feel ill, even when you are not involved in it?

5. Have you ever thought that you do not fit in with the people around you?

6. Do crowds drain away from your energy?

7. Have you ever felt the need to isolate yourself from others in order to regain your energy?

8. Do you get overwhelmed or overstimulated when you hear loud noises?

9. Do you get overwhelmed or overstimulated when you smell strong odors, regardless of whether the odor is pleasant or not?

10. Do you get overwhelmed or overstimulated when you are around people who talk incessantly?

11. Do you get overwhelmed or overstimulated whenever you wear clothes made of itchy fabric?

12. Do you have the tendency to binge with food and/or drinks in order to cope with stress or pain?

13. Does your body react strongly to caffeinated drinks?

14. Does your body react strongly to the side effects of the medication you are taking?

15. Does the concept of intimate relationships with other people make you feel uneasy?

16. Does your spouse or intimate partner often make you feel suffocated?

17. Are you easy to startle?

18. Do you have a low threshold for pain?

19. Have you ever observed yourself absorbing the stress felt by those around you?

20. Have you ever observed yourself absorbing the emotions felt by those around you?

21. Do you prefer doing your tasks one at a time instead of multitasking?

22. Do you regenerate your energy by going out for walks or hikes?

23. Do you need a long time to regain your energy after spending time with energy vampires?

24. Do you prefer living in a small town rather than in big cities?

25. Do you prefer engaging with a few people only rather than joining a large gathering of people?

Once you have answered each question, get the total number of "yes" responses you have given. Decode the meaning by matching your total with the following:

- 1 to 7 "yes" responses: You have a low level of empathy.

- 8 to 12 "yes" responses: You are exhibiting signs of moderate empathic abilities.

- 13 to 17 "yes" responses: You have a high level of empathy.

- 17 to 25 "yes" responses: You are a full-fledged empath.

Getting a confirmation that you are an empath is an important step in taking control over your special abilities. Instead of simply wondering whether your experiences are signs of being an empath, you have taken a proactive approach by going through the guide questions given above. From here on, you would be able to form better means of self-care and improve your relationships with those you care about.

Chapter 6 – The Differences between Sensitive People and Empaths

Some literature on empathy use the terms "sensitive person" and "empath" interchangeably. This is inaccurate for there are key differences between these two types of people. The confusion is understandable, however. According to experts, all empaths are sensitive, but not all sensitive people possess the gift of empathy.

To further elaborate the differences, here are the key distinctions that separate one from the other:

- Sensitivity

    Sensitive people are highly aware of their surroundings, even of the subtle changes that average individuals overlook. Because of this, they can easily be overwhelmed by the large amounts of stimuli that are beyond their control.

    These traits are also present among empaths. However, their level of sensitivity goes beyond their physical senses. Empaths pick up the emotions and energies of the people around them and then take them on as if they were their own. They literally experience whatever the other person is feeling. As such, they can get overwhelmed not just by their surroundings, but also by the strong emotions felt by people nearby.

- Processing of Highly Emotional Situations

Sensitive people can get affected by the extremely positive and negative emotions of others. For example, they feel miserable when a friend suffers from a tragedy. They do not, however, feel the same level of pain and despair as the other person does. What they are feeling is their own pain from seeing others in such a state. The emotions are their own, though it has been triggered by an external factor.

Empaths, on the other hand, would go through the experience as they are personally going through the same tragedy. Aside from misery and pain, they would also absorb the anxiety, physical pain, and stress levels of the other person. If they would or could not remove themselves from that situation, the empath would exhibit the same emotions and pains as the other person does. For example, if the person gets a migraine from crying, the empath would also develop a migraine just because they are nearby that grieving person.

- Ability to Read the Emotions of Other People

    Because they are feeling their own emotions, sensitive people tend to view others through the lens of how they are feeling now. They do not completely understand where the other person is coming from, or why the person is feeling happy, sad, or upset. Instead, they project their personal issues on others and assume what others might be feeling based on they would react if they were in that situation.

    In comparison, empaths are inherently sensitive towards non-verbal cues that give away the true emotions of other people. Over time and with regular practice, they can be effective at reading between the lines, especially when one's words do not match the emotions that are being picked up by the empath. Instead of projecting outwards, empath draws in the emotions of others and process them accordingly.

To clarify, empaths and sensitive people differ primarily on their capability to pick up and understand the emotions of others. Though every empath is also considered as sensitive, not all sensitive people are empaths as well. Therefore, before you label yourself as an empath, check first if you possess the general qualities observed among empaths.

Chapter 7 – Everything You Need to Know about Empath's Personality Type

Like emotionally average individuals, empaths possess and exhibit a wide variety of personality traits. These characteristics tend to express themselves in groups, which led experts to believe that there are certain personality types that are primarily associated with this special ability.

Here is a rundown of the five main classifications of personality types that empaths might belong to:

a. "The Bridge"

Empaths with this personality type are natural mediators. They also seek to compromise rather than gain the upper hand and hurt the feelings of the other party in the process. Using their skills, they could effectively create bridges between diverging opinions of the people around them. This is made possible by the mindset of "the bridge", which is to resolve—not win—a given situation.

If you are to observe empaths from this category, you will notice that they also take the time to consider the points being made by every party involved. Should there be anything to clarify, they do not hesitate in asking the questions that would allow them to form viable options that would hopefully lead to compromise.

It should be noted that because of their role, they are likely to suffer from emotional burnouts. Exposing themselves to both sides of an argument doubles the number of emotions and negative energies that they might absorb from other people. As such, acts of self-care should form a significant part of their daily routine.

b. "The Cheerleader"

Optimistic is what best describes empaths that are classified as "the cheerleader." They tend to become highly energized whenever others achieve their respective goals, even if it cost the empath so much of their time and effort.

Empaths under this category view themselves as supporting characters to people who have great visions and dreams. They feel like they belong together as a team, so the other person's accomplishment can usually make them feel happy and fulfilled too.

c. "The Golden Retriever"

Experts suggest that empaths with this personality type are the loyal and one of the most trustworthy companions that anyone can have. "The golden retriever" is always there to back up the ones he or she cares about, no matter what the situation is. Because of this unwavering bond, empaths who exhibit this personality trait tend to simply accept the negative emotions and energies that may be deliberately or unintentionally directed at them.

Fortunately, most "golden retrievers" are adept at handling the challenges associated with being an empath. However, they might be receptive to the negativities of others, their coping mechanisms tend to be more effective than those possessed by other personality types might. This extraordinary trait allows them to see beyond one's flaws and mistakes, and focus instead on the other person's potential and good qualities.

d. "The Overly Considerate"

People who are with empathic individuals normally find themselves unable to keep their stories to themselves. They feel at ease, especially since certain empaths know when to nod their head in understanding, and what words to say to assure or console the people they are talking to.

Even when given a chance to interrupt, these empaths let others rant out and vent their emotions and thoughts. They are not doing because they do not have their own stories to tell. Empaths who possess "the overly considerate" personality type just tend to put the needs and wants of others first before their own. No matter how happy or sad they are feeling at that given moment, empaths under this category would always go last, in consideration to the other person they are with.

e. "The Big-Hearted"

According to the Myers-Briggs Type Indicator (MBTI), people who score high in Sensing and Feeling (SF) or Intuition and Feeling (NF) are most likely to possess the gift of empathy. Collectively, these people are known as "the big-hearted" empaths due to their caring and understanding nature.

Compared to the other types, empaths with this kind of personality are considered the warmest and friendliest. They like to extend out a helping hand even to strangers. Their incredible skills at communicating with others, coupled with their insightful observations, allow them to create friendships and be of service to others wherever they go.

Majority of empaths fall into either one of these five personality types, or a combination of two or more types. Though their empathic abilities manifest in different ways, the defining characteristic of empaths remains consistent across every type.

This is what truly separates empaths from those who lack the special ability to establish deep and strong emotional connections with those around them.

Chapter 8 – The Main Empath Traits

The hallmark of an empath is the ability to feel, absorb, and understand the emotions, and, to some extent, the thoughts of the people around them. However, using this general statement as a basis of determining one's likelihood of being an empath is not enough. You also have to examine if you or the person you are evaluating possesses the following main traits of empathic individuals.

a. Extremely sensitive

Sensitivity among empaths come in two forms. First, their sense of smell and hearing tend to be more acute than normal people. They can easily get overwhelmed by strong odors, loud noises, and people who talk incessantly.

Second, their sensitive nature makes them easily affected by the words and emotions of other people. They are inherently good listeners, but sometimes to a fault. Their openness towards others leaves them vulnerable towards being taken advantage of or being hurt by the people around them.

b. Highly Intuitive

Through intuition, empaths are able to figure out who would be ideal companions for them. Listening to their guts allow them to avoid being stuck with energy vampires and toxic people. Trusting their intuition, however, takes time and practice, even though empaths typically possess this trait upon birth.

c. Caring

Empaths generally have a soft spot for those who are in need. Seeing scenes of misery and helplessness tug at their heartstrings. However, instead of just finding ways to help out, empaths feel the suffering and pain of others as if they were their own.

Caring, for empaths, is not simply reaching out to a homeless man who is starving and parched. They would feel intensely the ache and distress of that man, causing them to feel upset even if they were fine just a moment ago. That is why empaths try to make others feel better, whether or not they will get something back in return.

d. Emotionally absorptive

An empath's emotions are only as good as the emotions of those around them. If their companions are feeling happy and motivated, the empath would absorb these positive vibes, and adapt similar feelings as well. However, if the people nearby are feeling despondent, the empath's emotions would reflect the same mood.

Sometimes, empaths do not simply absorb the emotions of other people. Since they also have their own emotions, the energy and feelings they absorb become more intensified. For instance, instead of feeling happy and motivated just like the people around them, empaths could end up feeling ecstatic and enthusiastic. The same principle applies to negative emotions.

e. Introverted

Because of their sensitive and absorptive nature, empaths prefer to be alone or to be with a small group only. Even if the empath is on the more extraverted side of the spectrum, they impose limits on how many parties and social gatherings they would go to, and how long they are going to stay there.

If they need to recharge, empaths look for opportunities to escape. By doing so, they would prevent themselves from being emotionally and physically burnt out.

f. Overwhelmed by intimacy

Too much intimacy with another person can be challenging for empaths. Because they tend to absorb the feelings of those around them, most empaths fear that they will be influenced too much by their partner, causing lose their identity eventually. It is possible for them to be in a healthy intimate relationship as long as their partner is willing to understand their needs and compromise along the way.

g. Attuned with nature

Everyday life can be exhausting for empaths. They have to deal with different emotions and demands of the people around them. As such, they relish time spent out in nature where they can be alone and regain their focus and energy. Hiking, camping, or going to the beach are some of the outdoor activities that many empaths enjoy doing.

Being an empath can be a gift or a curse, depending on how one would look at it. Examining the traits possessed by people with this special ability provides good points for either side of the argument. Therefore, it is now in the hands of the empaths themselves on how they are going to make the most out of the positive traits and handle the negative traits associated with empathy.

Chapter 9 – How to Develop Your Gifts and Talents

To develop the gifts and talents of empaths, experts recommend a two-step approach: read properly the emotions of others, and show how much you understand them. Take note that each step is dependent on one another. By doing these steps as a cyclic process, you would be able to significantly improve your empathic abilities.

Reading the Emotions of Other People

The first aspect of empathy that you can develop is your ability to read and understand the emotions of those around you. There are numerous ways on how you could go about this, but the main goal for every one of them is to gain an awareness of how another person might be feeling. Though reading the emotions of others is not an exact science—given the complexities of human nature—you would still be able to get valuable information that would help you learn how to act and think like a highly empathic individual.

To truly understand other people, you need to have the ability to recognize where they are coming from and figure out how they think and feel. Showing others that you are capable of this is usually a disarming experience for them. When you manage to disarm them, they would be more likely to take off their masks and share with you their real thoughts and feelings. Only then would you be able to offer the help that they actually need from others.

In a way, highly empathic individuals are selfless beings. They step out of their comfort zones to totally immerse themselves in the lives of other people. They are willing to open up themselves in order to figure out how to make things better for those around them.

So, how would you be able to walk in the shoes of another person? One of the most recommended methods by experts is a three-prong approach. The main objective, however, is to read between the lines. Listen to what others have to say, but focus on how they are saying it. By doing this, you would be able to get a more accurate image of the person before you.

- Analyzing the Words of Other People

  Highly empathic individuals are effective listeners. They are able to pay attention to what the other person is saying, and from there, pick out the points that really matter. They are not just listening to what others have to say. They are also processing as well as the information that they are receiving at the same moment.

  There are times when words do not align with what the other person truly means. As such, empath needs to figure out what the other person is hinting at. Taking your listening skills to the next level needs time and practice. To make this process easier for you, do this exercise with someone you already know, and who is willing to tell you if your observations are accurate or not.

  - First, let your partner speak about whatever topic that he or she wants to talk about at that given moment. Do not converse with your partner. Instead, just focus and listen to what they have to say.

    For example, your partner, Anna, chooses to talk about her personal issues with her husband, Ben. Apparently, Anna wants to have kids, but Ben does not. Anna says that at first, it bothered her, but now she thinks it does not matter anymore.

o As you listen to her, take note of any emotion seeping through the tone of her voice. Check if there is any contradiction between her tone and the words, she is saying.

Following the same scenario given above, when Anna said that the issue is not bothering her anymore, you picked up the disappointment in the tone of her voice. Your ears heard her words correctly, but your intuition as an empath tells you that there is something else going on.

o Reflect on the meaning of the words of your partner, and analyze them against the tone of her voice. Given the melody and rhythm of her voice, you believe that Anna still wants to have to kids and that she feels frustrated over her husband's refusal to have them in the future.

You can empathize with her by acknowledging her true feelings. Do not question the accuracy of her words. Instead, focus on what she truly feels to show that you understand the underlying meaning of her words.

When you have managed to say something back that correctly reflects the true meaning of your partner's words, the relationship between the two of you becomes closer. A deeper bond would begin to form since your partner would believe that you get where she is coming from. Continue practicing your skills as an intuitive listener so that you would be able to form more accurate conclusions about what people truly mean with their words.

- Understanding the Facial Expressions of Other People

Speaking to another person involves not only your ears but also your eyes. You have to observe the facial cues in order to get a fuller understanding of what others are saying. Even when someone is silent, their faces usually give away what they are really thinking or feeling at a given moment.

To help you practice this skill, here is a list of facial features that you need to observe, and the corresponding meanings of the common expressions that you might notice as you do so.

- Eyes

    The eyes are a good source of information for empaths since most of its movements are automatic responses rather than controlled or deliberate. By observing them, you would be able to get a better idea of where the other person is coming from.

    If a person's gaze is steady and does not back away when you stare back at him or her, then the person is likely not hiding anything away from you. If you two are conversing, then he or she believes in what you are saying.

    On the other hand, a person who averts his or her gaze from you is most likely feeling worried about something. That person may also be hiding something, and he or she feels anxious that you would be able to uncover it. If someone's gaze shifts away whenever you make eye contact with him or her, it could either be an act of anxiety or avoidance.

- Eyebrows

  The position of the eyebrows is indicative of a person's feelings. According to experts, human eyebrows move not only when the person is feeling happy or sad, but also whenever someone feels an extreme emotion in reaction to stimuli or information.

  For instance, when the eyebrows are raised, the person could either be feeling surprised or curious. However, depending on the context of the situation, this position could also be taken as a sign of relief.

  If the eyebrows are lowered, it could mean either that the person is experiencing displeasure, or that the person is trying to hide away something from others. The position is seen as an unintentional act of hiding one's gaze, similar to when the eyes dart away from the gaze of other people.

- Forehead

  Check if the forehead of the person you are observing is wrinkled or smooth. If someone is deep in thought or confused, the forehead tends to become wrinkled. Smooth foreheads indicate that the person is feeling at ease or unbothered.

Signs of sweating on the forehead are also something that you should look out for. If the weather is not particularly warm, sweating on the forehead or any other part of the face could mean that the person is feeling anxious.

o Mouth

Observe if the person is exhibiting signs of a smile or frown. This is pretty telling of a person's true emotions, not just, because smiles and frowns are usually associated with happiness and sadness, respectively. If the emotion expressed in the eyes and mouth do not match, then the person is likely trying to hide his or her true feelings about someone or a certain situation.

To increase your level of empathy, try to practice reading the facial expressions of someone who can tell how accurate you are. However, please note that any variances between the expression and the words of a person do not mean that the person is deliberately doing it. Sometimes, a person is unaware of their facial expressions or what they are truly feeling.

Explaining how you have come about your conclusions is a more effective approach. Rather stating it like a fact, it would also be helpful if you would adopt a questioning tone when you try to assess someone's facial expressions. Here are some following guide questions that you could use for this:

- o Are you feeling anxious right now?

- o Do you feel happy about that?

- o Is that bothering you?

- o Do my words upset you?

- Decoding the Body Language of Other People

Beyond one's facial expression, a person's body language is also a veritable source of information for empaths. People with high levels of empathy are able to turn this information into a deeper understanding of the people around them.

Here is a list of tips on how you can effectively decode the meanings of one's bodily gestures:

- o If a person is feeling comfortable or dominant, he or she would usually adopt an open posture—head is held up; the body is facing forward; arms extended outwards, or arms kept at the person's sides).

- A person who feels inferior exhibits a closed body posture, wherein he or she has her arms folded while facing away.

- A person leaning forwards shows that he or she is interested. If coupled with a tense body, it could mean that the person is feeling angry instead.

- If the shoulders are drooping, the person is likely feeling sad or tired.

- A body that is facing away can be indicative of a person's anxiety, embarrassment, or shyness.

- One can adopt a welcoming posture by standing or sitting with arms opened up towards other people.

- On the other hand, arms crossed in front of the body signals that the person is feeling defensive over something or towards someone.

Showing Others That You Understand Their Feelings

The other empathic ability that you can develop is your ability to show others that you understand their feelings. The timing and the manner of expressing this separates a highly empathic person from other people with average or low empathy.

Again, it is best to practice this with a person that you are close with. Learn how to pace yourself as well. Starting too intensely would make the other person feel uncomfortable. You can try to practice first with minor inconveniences of day-to-day to life.

- Checking in with Other People

  The next step after assessing the emotions of another person is to check how accurate you are. By doing so, you would be able to better direct your growth as an empathic person. You may check-in with other people by phrasing it as either a statement or a question. Read the following examples to get a better sense of how to do this properly:

  o You look like you are feeling happy.

  o You seem to be in a sad mood.

  o You appear as if you are worried.

  o You seem like a confident person.

  o Are you in pain?

  o Do you feel happy about your accomplishment?

  o Is something making you feel embarrassed?

  o How lonely have you been feeling these past few days?

- Getting Confirmation from Other People

  It is not enough for you to gain an understanding of the inner thoughts and emotions of other people. You need to get feedback from the people you are reading so that you can keep track of your growth and development as an empath.

  By asking the right question or making an accurate statement, the other person would be able to confirm the observations you have made about him or her. If it is not entirely correct, then request for more detailed feedback on which parts you have gotten wrong.

  Do not be disheartened if you failed to produce good results at the start. It is perfectly acceptable since reading the emotions of others does not come naturally. It is a skill that you have to study and practice in order to gain complete mastery over this.

Developing your gifts and talents, as an empath is an achievable feat as long as you remain focused and dedicated to your goals. Aside from regular practice, you should also recognize the value of checking in and getting confirmation. It is better to learn what you are getting right and which points need further improvement. Doing so would save you a lot of time and effort.

Chapter 10 – How Negative Energy Directly Impacts on an Empath

Possessing the gift of empathy has its benefits and drawbacks, especially when the empath has not learned or developed adequate defense and coping mechanisms against negative energy. When this happens, empaths would likely experience struggles in their day-to-day life.

While many believe that being an empath is a blessing, it comes with a cost to the person bearing it. Some of the common issues they face include depression, anxiety, physical pain, and burnout. Furthermore, if their deficiencies are not properly addressed, empaths could come across as needy or lazy.

These effects of negative energy have a significant impact on the life of an empath. Here is a list of areas wherein empaths could have trouble with when they let negativity rule over them.

1. Watching movies or TV shows

   Due to the prevalent themes of violence and cruelty in the media, empaths cannot simply watch any movie or TV show. Many people find this activity as relaxing and entertaining, especially at the end of a long day. Empaths cannot indulge themselves since emotional scenes would only drain off whatever remains of their energy.

2. Keeping a job

Empaths excel at their jobs when they enjoy what they are doing. However, the moment the tasks become too tedious or boring for them, they usually quit and look for something else. This stems from their tendency to feel things more intensely than average people do. It is normal for someone to feel moments of doubt or helplessness, even if one loves his or her job. Empaths, unfortunately, take these moments into another level. Because of this, inexperienced empaths find it hard to achieve professional success in their chosen fields.

3. Maintaining relationships

There are various struggles faced by empaths whenever they are in a relationship with other people. First, they have this perennial need to escape and be alone, especially when they are exhausted or overwhelmed. In some cases, empaths could not even sleep on a bed with another person because they would end up not getting any rest at all. If their partner does not understand or respect their reasons for avoiding intimacy at certain times, the relationship between them would surely suffer.

Another source of the problem in empaths' relationships is their ability to tell if someone is lying to them. Due to their sensitive and perceptive nature, even harmless white lies do not go undetected. Lying, even in normal relationships, causes friction between the couple. The resulting hurt and disappointment are further intensified among empaths.

4. Developing addictive habits

Empaths are always seeking ways to effectively block out the emotions of others. Because of this need to protect themselves, some empaths might feel desperate enough to resort to unhealthy forms of escape. This includes, but are not limited to alcohol, drugs, and sex. In their attempt to find a way out, they become stuck in a self-destructive cycle instead.

Being an empath is not easy. They experience problems in their personal, social, and work lives that normal people do not have to deal with on a regular basis. Learning the difficulties of having this ability is essential not only for the empaths themselves but for the people around them as well. Only then would everyone appreciate this special and multi-faceted gift.

Chapter 11 – How to Protect Yourself from Energy Vampires

Empaths are highly vulnerable to extreme conditions and emotions felt by other people. This is further exacerbated by the so-called energy vampires who feed off the energy of individuals near them. Other characteristics observed among energy vampires include:

- a negative mindset

- selfish and self-obsessed

- overly critical

- controlling over others

- likes to gossip around

To combat the negative effects of being exposed to them, empaths could employ the following means of protecting themselves from such attacks:

Step #1: Determine if you are in the presence of an energy vampire.

Experiencing at least one of the following symptoms, without any other probable cause, could indicate that your energy is being sapped away by another person.

- o Your mood drops down even if you were feeling fine a moment ago.

- o You are on edge since everything seems to agitate you.

- o You suddenly crave for carbs or your go-to comfort food.

- o Your eyelids grow heavier by the minute.

- o You yawn as frequently as when you need to take a nap.

Step #2: Remember and comply with these dos and don'ts on dealing with energy vampires.

Once you have confirmed that you are with an energy vampire, the ideal protective measure is to get away from them immediately, but without provoking them even further. However, there are cases wherein this is not entirely possible—for instance if he or she is a family member who lives in the same house as you.

To save you from suffering, follow these tips on how to effectively deal with energy vampires.

Do:

- Take deep breaths for a few minutes to center yourself.

- Trust and listen to your intuition especially when it is signaling you of impending danger or harm.

- Stay levelheaded even if they are trying to bait you with incendiary remarks or questions.

- Pause and think of ways to escape from the situation.

- Use a neutral tone to communicate your discomfort and boundaries.

Do not:

- Ignore what your inner voice is telling you.

- Label yourself as "neurotic" for being uncomfortable in their presence.

- Fight physically and/or verbally with the energy vampire.

- Binge-eat or drink to alleviate the side effects that you are feeling.

- Show signs of fear or submission.

As an empath, you are not obliged to rehabilitate energy vampires. Leave that task to themselves and mental health professionals. What you should focus on is protecting yourself from them. Keep in mind, however, that energy vampires are people who deserve your understanding and compassion too. Though you would have to set boundaries between you and them, always try to remain polite and respectful to avoid hurting them unnecessarily.

Chapter 12 – Methods to Fight Negative Energy

Empaths who have just recently recognized their special gifts for what they really tend to ask this question: how can an empath fight off the negative energy and vibes from the people around them? The naive answer to this is by attempting to turn yourself into this paragon of happiness and optimism.

There is more to this question than a simple idealized version of what an empath should be. If you believe that you are an empath, you need to learn how to properly and adequately defend yourself since the other options are neither healthy nor tempting.

Here is a list of effective strategies that you can play whenever you feel the symptoms of a negativity build-up in your own system. The best way to find out which ones would work for you is to mix it up and experiment. No one strategy is objectively better than the rest. It is all a matter of finding out which one would fit your lifestyle and still effectively address your concerns as an empath.

Strategy #1: Take a minute and determine the source of your symptom.

Identifying the source of your pain and distress is a valuable strategy because only then would you be able to formulate an effective plan to alleviate the symptoms or any discomfort that you are feeling. One of the most noticeable signs that the negative energy or emotion has originated from another person is a sudden change in your physical condition or mood while you are in the presence of the said person. Remember, whenever you feel anxious, sad, or exhausted, there would always be a chance that your distress is caused—to a certain extent—by the person close to you now.

To confirm if this is the case for you, simply step away from them for a brief moment. Observe yourself and see if the symptoms you were feeling earlier would remain or dissipate. The latter means that the negativity is definitely not yours.

In some cases, however, the symptoms stem from a combination of your feelings and those around you. This is more likely to happen when the root cause of the negativity within you bears similarities with the person you are with.

For example, empaths who are confined in a hospital due to sickness are susceptible to catching on the stress and pain of others since the empath is personally suffering health-wise. In cases like this, the empath may have to resort to other strategies since stepping away from the contributors to your suffering is not an option.

Strategy #2: Breathe and repeat a mantra similar to this: "Release me from this suffering."

If you feel that negative energy is starting to overwhelm you, take a short pause and focus on your breathing. Feel the air flowing through your system as you breathe in and out. Continue to do so for the next few minutes until you could feel the negative energy flowing out of your body.

Should you feel like the negativity is stuck within you, hold your breath for a few seconds and imagine the stress and discomfort you are feeling turn into a ball of energy in the middle of your chest. Resume your breathing as you continue to envision this image inside your head.

After a minute or two, repeat under your breath this mantra: "Release me from this suffering." As you say this, imagine the ball of negative energy floating away from your chest. Do not picture it returning to the origin since it would be unkind to do so. Though it would not actually be returned to that person, thinking that way is counterintuitive since it would only attract more negative energy towards you.

Strategy #3: Maintain a comfortable, but a polite distance away from the cause of your discomfort.

This strategy is easier to pull off when you are in the presence of strangers. According to experts, the optimal distance is around twenty feet or six meters. If you are in a public place, such as a movie theater or public transport, consider changing seats if that is a possible option at that given moment.

If the person sitting next to you does not make you feel comfortable, spare yourself from the suffering. Get up from your seat, and find a more suitable spot for you. Remember, self-care is just as important as being careful about the feelings of others.

Do not make a big deal whenever you have to do so. Practice subtlety to not offend the people around you. Empaths run the risk of exposing themselves to social situations that can overwhelm both their bodies and minds. If you would ever be put in that situation, leave as quietly as possible and maintain a comfortable distance from the possible sources of negativity around you.

Strategy #4: Limit eye contact and/or physical contact with other people.

Certain research studies suggest that energy can be transmitted through gaze or touch. Therefore, if you are not feeling comfortable at any given moment, try to limit the eye contact or physical contact you have with those around you.

For example, many people prefer to greet others with a hug. It is perfectly all right to refuse a friendly hug, as long as you express it in a polite manner. If you are not the position to deny it, try to shorten the duration of the hug as much as possible. You can also go for a half-hug instead, wherein you just pat someone on the back after wrapping an arm around him or her. Always keep in mind that you have the right to choose the amount of eye contact or physical contact you would engage in with others.

Some people express their sympathies through a hug or some other thoughtful gesture. Studies indicate that hugging does benefit both the giver and recipient emotionally. However, if you are concerned about the effect it would have on your stress level, there are many other ways to show how much you care about them, even from a safe, but polite distance.

Strategy #5: Use water to detox yourself.

One of the quick techniques employed by many empaths is water immersion, or in non-technical language, taking a long, hot bath. To make it more effective, some throw in Epsom salt into the water in order to induce a more calming atmosphere.

Essential oils are also indispensable when it comes to relaxing baths. Many empaths use lavender oils in particular due to its calming properties.

When in need of intensive pampering, some people with empathic abilities travel to places with natural mineral springs. The pure water found in those springs is believed to be capable of detoxing both the body and the mind.

Strategy #6: Learn how and when to say "no."

To survive and thrive as an empath, one must learn how to set his or her limits and boundaries. If being with someone drains away from your energy, do not simply suffer in silence. You have complete control over how much time you would spend with that person. If you have been invited to hang out with them again, learn how to say "no"—with or without further explanation.

If you do want to keep the relationship for whatever reason, try to express your preferences and needs to that person. It is better to be upfront about it early on in order to avoid any misunderstanding between the two of you.

Another example of where you could draw the line is deciding upon whether or not you would accept an invitation to go out and spend time with other people. If you are not in the mood for a party, turn down the invitation. You may explain yourself, but remember that you are not obliged to do so. Just learn how to be consistent about your limits and boundaries in order to avoid sending out the wrong message to those around you.

Strategy #7: Use visualization techniques.

Visualization has been proven an effective way of achieving something with the power of your mind. In this case, if you feel that you are being affected too much by someone else's negative energy, visualize a cord connecting you to them. This could be stemming out from anywhere in your body, but most people imagine it coming out of their chests or stomachs.

When the image becomes clearer inside your head, think about how you are going to cut that cord. Most of the time, people use either a scissor or a knife. Keep in mind that you are going to completely cut off your relationship with that person. You only wish to eliminate the unpleasant energies that you are drawing or receiving from him or her.

Once you are ready, use your knife or scissors to cut the cord between the two of you. Imagine a sense of relief washing down your system. Spend a few more minutes meditating until you are ready to go on with the rest of your day.

This technique is usually employed by those who feel drained by their loved ones. Those empaths wish to retain the good parts of their relationships, so they focus instead on finding out ways on how to turn down or eliminate the negative effects of their loved one's energy and emotions on them.

Strategy #8: Schedule alone time on a regular basis.

Most empaths recognize the value of spending time alone. If you plan to use this as a way to regain your energy, then you should plan and make room for this in your schedule.

One technique to make this more effective is turning off your personal devices, such as cellphones, tablets, and laptops. Do not think about the messages or calls that you might be missing at that moment. Focus on your thoughts and emotions instead.

You do not have to clear your whole day for your alone time. This could be done in at least one hour, but if you need to recharge more, then you probably could go up to a half-day for this. Ideally, you know your needs better than anyone do, so listen to what your inner self has to say about the concept of regaining energy by spending time alone.

Strategy #9: Ground yourself by spending time out in nature.

Nature has a way of making empaths feel at ease. Natural bodies of water coupled with beautiful green scenery can induce relaxation and calm among empaths. It is also said that our planet's electromagnetic fields have healing capabilities. Therefore, empaths could try to refresh themselves by lying down in a quiet meadow and soak up the planetary energies emanating from the ground.

Referred to as earthling, walking on your bare feet is believed to be a healing practice by some spirituality experts. It could be done on a lawn, or on a sandy beach. The concept is simple that many empaths practice this even in the comforts of their own homes.

You can combine this strategy with the previous one. At least once a year, set aside time for a personal retreat. It should be an activity that you could do on your own or with a minimal number of companions. The primary objective of your retreat is to decompress and recalibrate your system. By doing so, you would gain back your energy, and hopefully, a fresh perspective on things that matter most to you.

Strategy #10: Take power naps or sleep for at least six to seven hours per day.

Sleeping is the body's natural way of gaining back the strength and energy to go on the next day. Empaths benefit from a restful sleep or nap since it also calms down their nerves. They absorb stress and emotions all throughout the day, which makes them, feel exhausted by night.

Sleeping seven to eight hours per day is usually enough, but there are certain times when you need more time to rest. Indulge yourself by sleeping in early or staying for one more hour in bed—if you are not missing other important activities or other responsibilities. Taking brief power naps during the daytime has also been proven to be healing for empaths.

Strategy #11: Step away from social media platforms and the news.

A regular timeout from social media and the news is a necessary part of self-care routines for empaths. The content from those websites and the news of the day are observed to be likely triggers to the intense emotional reactions of empaths.

Contrary to popular belief, empaths do not need to actually see or be with another person to absorb his or her energy. Reading their posts or listening to the news about the sufferings of other people are more than enough to cause a negative impact on the wellbeing of an empath.

Therefore, you should include in your schedule a "social media and news fasting" every week. This means that you would completely avoid browsing through your feeds. The television would have to be turned off to block whatever breaking news might disrupt your regular shows.

Another method is to avoid using social media platforms or watching the news before going to bed. By doing so, you would be able to sleep better, which would ultimately do wonders to your physical and mental health.

Strategy #12: Meditate.

When it comes to negative energy, many empaths find meditation as one of the most valuable tools to combat stress and other disruptive environmental factors. Fortunately, you do not have to allow significant time for this activity. You could simply learn quick meditation techniques, and then practice them whenever you are feeling overwhelmed or tired.

As you meditate, try to refocus your mind on yourself only. Do not think about other people or your responsibilities. Aim to forge a healthy and loving relationship with your own body and mind. You need a strong connection between the two because you cannot successfully ward off negative energy with only just one of them. When you have achieved this feat, you will be able to better protect yourself from the harmful effects of interacting with different types of people every day.

Chapter 13 – Emotional Intelligence

Over the years, psychologists have come up with different definitions of emotional intelligence. Though the details vary from one expert to another, the consensus is that this type of intelligence appears to be almost non-existent among certain people who are book smart. Those people can solve complex mathematical problems or win debates through their careful research and ingenious arguments. However, when it comes to emotional control and awareness of others and their own selves, the book smart people seem to be lacking compared to those with only average grades but have higher levels of the so-called street smarts. This phenomenon gave rise to the notion that some other forms of intelligence exist besides what can be taught through books and classrooms.

Components of Emotional Intelligence

The following five abilities define emotionally intelligent individuals:

- Empathy

  This refers to the ability of a person to feel and understand the emotions of those around them in a deeper and more personal level, thus prompting the person to reach out and help those in need.

- Motivation

  A person is motivated when he or she strives to grow, improve, and achieve excellence in whatever they are doing.

- Self-Awareness

  Self-aware individuals recognize their own emotions, and how these emotions can affect their thoughts and actions.

- Self-Regulations

  People who can self-regulate are able to handle their emotions in an appropriate manner, control their impulses, and adapt to changes in their environment.

- Social Skills

  If someone can effectively collaborate, communicate, and inspire others, then that person is said to have good social skills.

Traits Associated with High Emotional Intelligence

Ben, a high school student, struggles to achieve respectable grades in grammar and literature. Getting a C on an essay is a challenge for him, and yet, he can converse well with his peers and teachers alike. He belongs to a large group of friends, and he gets an invite to almost every party. Other students enjoy spending lunch breaks with him, and teachers and other parents like him well enough due to his polite and affable nature. By the time of his graduation, Ben manages to make all the right decisions and gets himself into a great university, despite his academic struggles.

This scenario may sound familiar to you. It could be someone you know, or it could also be you, to a certain extent. Whichever the case may be, it is apparent that this is not a rare case of extreme luck or divine providence. Some may ascribe Ben's situation to either of those probabilities, but it can be argued that his achievements in life are actually products of his high emotional intelligence.

To get a better picture of what emotional intelligence is, here are the common traits observed among people who are considered as street smart:

- Possess the right communication skills that allow them to express themselves in a clear manner

- Can recognize and regulate their emotional reactions toward a situation or another person

- Able to gain other's respect without demanding or begging for it

- Considered as influential by the people around them

- Know the right thing to say in order to get the results that they want

- Able to successfully elicit help from others whenever they need assistance

- Can effectively manage difficult situations

- Able to keep their cool when they are under pressure

- Effective at negotiating for good—or even better—terms

- Can motivate their own selves in order to get things done

- Able to keep a positive attitude especially during tough times

These traits do not strictly follow a single definition of emotional intelligence. Instead, these are the common behaviors and capabilities observed among people with reported high emotional intelligence. If this profile sounds too good to be true, keep in mind that like other forms of intelligence, emotional intelligence can be honed and improved upon through practice.

Chapter 14 – The Power of Emotional Intelligence

Nowadays, more and more companies and organizations are discovering the advantage of possessing emotional intelligence over academic prowess or, depending on the field, practical knowledge. This growing interest stems from the large wave of research studies conducted to shed light on the mystery that used to surround this concept.

Some are still hesitant to accept the merits of emotional intelligence, believing that unlike other learned skills, one must be born with high EQ. For them, it is something that discriminates against those who have not won the genetic lottery. However, as studies have shown repeatedly, this kind of thinking is nothing but a myth that has already been dispelled.

Compared to IQ, which usually remains on the same level, emotional intelligence can be improved throughout one's lifetime. It is a learned skill, even though some may be born with a predisposition to exhibit the traits associated with emotional intelligence. Combined with adequate support and a nurturing environment, a person can reap the benefits of being emotionally intelligent.

The Value of Emotional Intelligence in the Workplace

You have already learned from the earlier chapters the positive impacts of emotional intelligence in one's personal growth and social interactions. Now, to better appreciate the advantages of having a high EQ, here are the main reasons behind the increasing popularity of emotional intelligence among leading companies and large organizations.

- According to a recent study published in the Harvard Business Review, around ninety percent of the achievements made by leaders are attributed more too strong emotional intelligence rather than business savvy or IQ.

- Research shows that emotional intelligence contributes positively to both the physical and mental health of a person.

- Strategies and techniques on conflict resolution are more effective when components of emotional intelligence have been factored into the policy and procedure.

- Friendly yet productive and ethical relationships between colleagues are made possible when both parties exhibit signs of high emotional intelligence.

- The more developed ones EQ is, the more control that person has over the different aspects of his or her life.

Given these, certain HR practitioners have identified the following key traits that are embodied by employees and leaders with high emotional intelligence:

a. Smart risk-taker

This employee can adapt to and manage changes within the workplace. Understanding the risks involved when making a change, he or she makes all the necessary precautions before executing the plan.

b. Highly self-aware

Employees who are self-aware know well their strengths and weaknesses, both in terms of their work expertise and their emotions as a person. As such, they do not let themselves be held back when there is something they could still do to overcome their challenges in their career.

c. Empathic

Empathic employees have the ability to relate strongly but appropriately with their peers, superiors, and/or subordinates. They feel and understand both the positive and negative emotions of those they work with, which then allow them to adjust themselves accordingly.

d. Curious

Born with an innate sense of wonder, these employees are interested in discovering the less-known aspects of their interests and field of work. Their curiosity also makes them more accepting of the differences that exist between one people to another. They are not quick to judge, opting to listen first and take time to process their thoughts before making any conclusion.

e. Optimistic

These employees tend to the glass-half-full most of the time. They are appreciative of what they have in life and grateful for their good fortune. Because they rarely rant and complain about their lives, they are pleasant to work with, whether as a member or a leader of the team.

f. Resilient

This becomes evident when an employee is faced with a failure, regardless of whether he or she has caused it or if it is out of their control. The ability to roll with the punches is highly valuable, especially in industries that deal with demanding clients with high expectations.

g. Balanced

Nowadays, being a workaholic is not something that is seen in a wholly positive light by companies and organizations. Due to the negative side effects of being one, especially in terms of physical health and mental wellbeing, living a balanced lifestyle is now considered as a necessary trait of model employees. Anyone who can juggle their career, quality time with family, friends and loved one and a self-care routine are considered as highly functional individuals who would surely become assets to the team.

Given these traits, one could say that all components of emotional intelligence are now considered as necessary to become successful in any given field. Fortunately, if you believe that you are lacking in any of these areas, you can bridge the gap by learning how to improve your skills as an emotionally intelligent being.

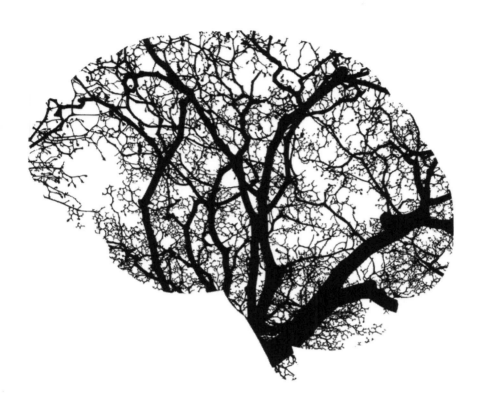

Chapter 15 – Managing Your Emotion

Having a bad day is entirely unavoidable for everyone. Days like that usually start with you feeling that something is off the moment you get up from your bed. It is usually accompanied by a mild headache or even hints of nausea. Everything seems to annoy you, and a feeling of dread continues to build up in your chest all throughout the day.

Some may be tempted to cancel all their plans, call in sick at work, and stay at home instead. However, this is not a healthy approach to such days, and most of the time, you cannot simply run away from your responsibilities. Because of this, you need to learn how to manage your emotions especially when things do not go your way.

Dealing with Negative Emotions

In general, having negative feelings is natural and needed in order to attain a balance in life. However, when the severity of these feelings become too much to handle, thereby causing you to lose focus and motivation, then you need to address them right away to avoid bigger problems later on.

Here are some techniques you can apply yourself in order to handle negative emotions. Keep in mind that these are only self-administered remedies to get you back on track with the rest of your day. You should seek the help of mental health professionals when none of the following techniques works for you.

- Cognitive Restructuring

First developed by Dr. Albert Ellis and Dr. Aaron Beck, this cognitive-behavioral technique is one of the most widely recommended by psychiatrists and therapists alike to their patients. The main principle behind this concept is that a person becomes what he or she thinks most of the time.

In terms of managing negative emotions, the primary goal is to dispute or replace cognitive distortions—or one's irrational beliefs about another person or a situation—with healthier and more accurate thoughts. Experts have recognized cognitive distortions as one of the main sources of negative emotions. Therefore, directly addressing them would be helpful in resolving a person is emotional and other personal issues, such as social anxiety, low self-esteem, and impulsiveness.

For major cases, it is best for them to go through this process with the aid of a professional. However, if you wish to handle things personally, first, here are the basic steps of cognitive restructuring:

1. Get yourself a personal journal or notebook where you can write down your thoughts and feelings during this exercise. Remember, it is best to go through this when you are alone, and in place that is free from any distraction.

2. Think of an event or time when you felt depressed, worried, stressed, or angry.

3. Using two pages of your personal journal, create a table with the following headings:

   a. Triggering Event

   b. Emotions Felt (During the Event)

   c. Initial Assumptions

   d. Positive Thoughts (About the Event)

   e. Negative Thoughts (About the Event)

   f. Balanced Thoughts (About the Event)

   g. Resulting Mood

   h. Action Plans

4. In the column for "Triggering Event", describe the situation that affected or is affecting negatively your mood.

5. Under the column for "Emotions Felt", specify your feelings during the event itself. Try to limit it to a single word only since anything longer would likely be an interpretation or your thoughts about the event rather than feelings.

6. For the "Initial Assumptions" column, indicate the thoughts that automatically came into your mind during the event itself.

7. Use the columns for "Positive Thoughts" and "Negative Thoughts" to respectively write down thoughts that dispute and contribute to your negative mood.

8. Taking into account what you have written on the preceding columns, form a conclusion that balances out the positive and negative aspects of the event. Write it down in the column for "Balanced Thoughts".

9. After having analyzed the event in a more objective manner, describe the current state of your mood in the "Resulting Mood" column.

10. Finally, formulate an action plan on how you see yourself moving forward from this.

Cognitive structuring is an effective tool that would help you work through emotionally difficult situations. Do not edit yourself as you write down your thoughts and feelings into your journal. The more honest you are with yourself, the more successful you would be in managing your emotions.

- Distraction

Classic advice given to people who feel overwhelmed by their responsibilities is to stay firm and confront your problems head-on. However, there are certain times when running away would actually be a healthier approach. In such cases, escaping for a bit—as long as you are not totally shirking your responsibilities—allows the person to breathe and realign their focus.

Depending on the complexity of the situation, you can apply this technique in various ways. You can simply pause whatever you are doing and slowly count from one to ten. However, if the situation really demands it, you can consider taking a much-needed vacation.

During your time away, you should try to reflect on your current situation. If you feel that your negative emotions have been escalating lately, take this time to sort out your feelings and cool your head.

There are many ways to distract yourself. Some of them are beneficial, while others are inherently harmful. Here is a list of quick ways to escape in a healthy manner:

- o Go out for a walk or run

- o Make lists of things that interest you

- o Exercise

- o Chat with someone you enjoy being with

- o Listen to your favorite music

- Meditation and Other Relaxation Activities

To feel more relaxed and calmer, an empath can use several techniques that would exercise both the body and mind. Doing these activities once would only be a short-term solution to your life-long need to manage your emotions. It would be best if you could incorporate these activities into your daily routine rather than use them as quick fixes to moments of personal crises.

These activities would not require much of your time. Most can be done in ten minutes—some, even less. When considered against the time you spend on your phone, watching the TV, or chatting with your friends, ten minutes would not require a big adjustment in your day-to-day schedule.

- Quick Exercise Routines

  Activities that require physical movements trigger the brain to release dopamine or the happiness hormone. Aside from turning up your mood, exercising has also been proven an effective technique to lower down one's stress level. In addition, gaining a sense of control over your body can boost your confidence, which in turn would improve your mental health as well.

- Belly Breathing

  When you breathe normally, air fills out your lungs, and the ribcage moves accordingly. According to experts, this movement contributes to the increase in your heart rate, which is one of the signs of building anxiety. This type of breathing has also been observed to intensify the emotions you are feeling at a given moment.

  In contrast, belly breathing requires you to restrict the movement of the ribcage when you breathe in and out. Instead, you let your diaphragm move to facilitate the airflow inside your lungs. The diaphragm is a muscle located between your lungs and stomach, and it is primarily utilized by musicians who play wind instruments since this technique allows more air to be retained in the lungs for a longer period compared to regular breathing.

Another advantage of belly breathing is that you can practice this wherever you are. Sitting, standing, or walking, you can breathe through your diaphragm to relieve you from the stress you are feeling at that moment.

- Acupressure

Following the same principles of the Shiatsu massage and acupuncture, acupressure is recommended by experts as an effective way of eliminating tension from your system. Though it sounds complicated, the steps to practice this are simple and easy to pull off:

1. Squeeze the area of the palm between your thumb and forefinger with the use of your thumb and forefinger of your other hand. Do not use extreme pressure. It should feel uncomfortable, not painful.

2. Count to five while maintaining this pressure on your hand.

3. Switch the positions of your hands, and repeat the first two steps.

4. Repeat this exercise for two more cycles.

5. Feel the tension dissipating from your body.

The techniques given above are short-term approaches to managing your emotions. In order to attain complete mastery over your emotions, you should consider making some personal changes in your attitude and behaviors. This means that rather than aiming to limit or minimize your feelings, your level of self-awareness is sufficient to let you control the timing and intensity of your emotions.

There are people who believe that emotions cannot be changed. These individuals let their emotions run free, whether they are feeling happy, sad, or angry. However, if you follow that kind of thinking, then you would never be able to take charge of your own life. What these people fail to understand is that depending on the situation, emotions can be changed, with or without one's conscious effort to do so.

Given the fickle nature of raw emotions, you should make an effort to control them for the sake of your personal growth and your relationship with other people. The key to achieving this feat is practice and a positive mindset.

- Practice

  Similar to playing a sport, techniques on managing your emotions require time and effort spent on practicing them. You cannot just walk into a basketball court, and expect to win when you have not played this sport for months.

  The same principle applies to whatever technique or strategy you have chosen for yourself. Set aside a regular time in your schedule and dedicate it to practicing your preferred methods of emotional coping.

  For example, you have observed that meditation works best for you. Include meditation into your daily routine. Pick the best time of day for this activity, given its requirement for a quiet place that is free from potential distractions. You do not have to limit yourself to one long session per day. Many people break this down into two quick bouts of meditation for each day. Figure out how it would fit into your schedule, and then stick to it.

For those who are always on the go, select techniques that you can do wherever you are or whatever you are doing. This includes belly breathing and acupressure. Say, for instance, you are lined up at the checkout counter of a grocery store. Practice your breathing, or apply acupressure on your hands while you wait for your turn. Pay no attention to the potential stressors in your environment. Instead, focus on improving yourself in terms of effectively managing your emotions.

- Positive Mindset

Positive psychology is one of the more recent movements in this field. Its main principles are centered on recognizing, understanding and celebrating one's strengths. As such, many experts on emotional intelligence believe that a positive mindset is one of the keys to managing one's emotions.

Most schools of thought in psychology are focused on studying the abnormalities and problems of the human mind. However, with the onset of positive psychology, the focus of many researchers has shifted to discovering and fostering the good aspects of the human psyche.

When you adopt a positive mindset, you would gain a fresh perspective on yourself. Rather than being bogged down by your perceived weaknesses and sensitivities, your attention would be on finding out your strengths and learning how to better make use of those strengths in improving yourself and those around you.

Hidden talents are more easily uncovered when you have positive regard about yourself. You are more willing to put yourself out there, and in doing so, you would have a greater chance of discovering aspects of yourself that no one—not even yourself—know about you before. Once recognized, you would then be able to focus on developing further your strengths.

As you continue pursuing them, these strengths and talents can lead you to figure out your true passion in life. You would then be able to find a career that best matches your personality and wants in life.

People who have managed to find the right path for them in life tend to be more emotionally mature and balanced. They feel contentment over their choices, and in turn, the people around feel their positive energy. You, too, can achieve this feat by learning ways to better manage your emotions and gain complete mastery over the emotional aspects of your being.

Chapter 16 – Understanding Others

One of the key elements of emotional intelligence is the capacity to understand others. Many associate it with empathy, which is one of the main abilities of an emotionally intelligent person. This means that this goes beyond merely sensing feelings and emotions. To understand others, you must take a genuine interest in them as individuals who think, feel, and experience things in their own way.

You are good at understanding others when you possess the following emotional and social skills:

- You can pick up and correctly interpret emotional cues.

  As you interact with others, you also automatically take note of the tone of their voice, facial expressions, body language, and other forms of non-verbal signals. Upon observing these cues, you can also make sense out of them, and figure out the meanings behind almost every expression and gesture you have noticed.

- You listen well to what the other person is saying.

  Listening does not only entail hearing every word said. It also requires a keen interest to understand what is being said, and an initiative to check if you got their message right. Without these elements, you are merely letting the words pass through one ear to the other.

- You exhibit sensitivity towards others.

Because emotionally intelligent people can see things from the perspective of others, they are more careful about their words and actions in case they inadvertently offend or hurt somebody. They are also respectful of others despite any differences between their opinions.

- You extend a helping hand to those in need.

Based on what you have picked up and what you understand about others, you are able to offer help in an appropriate manner. Your offer is also not empty words that lack the element of action. When you say you will help, others can rely on the integrity of your word.

Emotional Intelligence and Sincerity

One can pretend to understand others, particularly their concerns. Sometimes, this is one of the job requirements, such as those in the field of sales and customer service. They pretend to know exactly what the client is feeling so that they can establish and build rapport. However, humans are inherently capable of detecting lies, even ones that seem to be relatively harmless.

There are various ways to tell if one is being insincere. More often than not, it is the non-verbal cues that tend to give away one's attempts to cover up the truth. In some cases, responding to unexpected questions could also reveal one's intention to hide away certain things from others.

Even if a person were not, entirely aware of what is happening before him or her, a sense of discomfort would begin to grow, thereby drawing suspicion on the insincere party. This means that faking your way into seeming like an emotionally intelligent individual can be counterproductive to your goals. Learn how you can gain and develop genuine interest on others instead so that you would be able to better connect with the people around you.

Emotional Intelligence and Social Skills

Your ability to understand the feelings of other people and, in turn, your ability to manage your behaviors and emotions towards them reflect your emotional intelligence. Unless you have been living as a hermit, you care about the thoughts and feelings of those around, to a certain extent. Since almost everyone interacts with others on a regular basis, improving one's emotional intelligence can help a person achieve the following feats of effective social skills:

- Maintain healthy and satisfying relationships

- Find others who share similar interests

- Encourage others to regard you in a positive manner

- Ask for a favor from others without forcing them to accommodate your needs

- Convince another person to accept your idea or proposal

- Calm down a person who feels irate over significant or trivial matters

- Be of help to those in need

The last item on the list is particularly important since emotional intelligence is not just about the things that would benefit you. Learning how to pay attention to the needs and feelings of other people can have a significant impact on your growth as an emotionally intelligent person. Seeing things from others' perspective and, from there, figuring out how to react in an appropriate manner are signs of a person who is in touch with his own emotions.

Chapter 17 – Managing Your Relationship

Possessing an optimal level of emotional intelligence is an essential component of building relationships with those around you. As noted by researchers, people naturally gravitate towards emotionally intelligent individuals.

Think of the friends that you currently have. How many of them are unhappy, uncaring, or poor at communicating with others? Normally, those kinds of people do not have to belong to large groups of friends.

Creating Positive Friendly and Casual Relationships

More often than not, friendships are defined by one's level of emotional intelligence. It is not just a matter of shared interests. If the people within that relationship do not possess the necessary interpersonal skills to maintain their bond, the relationship is likely doomed to fail.

Other benefits that your friendships can reap from having good emotional and social skills include:

- Engage others in conversation

- Know which topics are appropriate and interesting for conversations

- Give sound personal advice

- Receive and process someone's advice for you

- Share personal stories about yourself

- Celebrate together important events in your life

Improving your interpersonal skills would allow you to grow your circle of friends and strengthen the bonds you have with your current friends. You would also be able to become more open to meeting new people. In turn, you will enjoy richer and more fulfilling life experiences.

Achieving Balance on Your Emotions and Social Interactions

Emotionally intelligent individuals are capable of finding the right balance in their interpersonal relationships. There are two ways on how one can fail at this:

- You might be too guarded, thus preventing people from getting close to you.

  This can be observed more frequently among couples wherein the male takes up a more traditional role. It is also a common trait among males where the social norms dictate large differences between gender roles.

- You might be too open about personal matters towards people who you have just met.

  Trying to get close to a stranger by disclosing your entire life history is counterintuitive to your goal of creating new relationships. They are likely going to be put off by your approach, thereby negating your attempts to make a real connection with them.

Knowing how to achieve the right balance between your emotions and social skills is a valuable skill to have. For some people, it comes naturally as part of their personalities. However, there are also certain people who just pick this up by observing others or watching characters in a movie or TV show. Take note that there are certain risks associated with this technique since not all forms of media attempt to highlight good approaches from poor ones. As such, it is still important to get proper guidance from experts and reputable literature on how you could create and maintain relationships with those around you.

Evaluating Your Intimate Relationships

According to experts, high emotional intelligence contributes to satisfying and healthy relationships. You can tell if you and your partner belong to such a relationship if:

- Both of you consider yourselves as good—if not best—friends.

- Your interests and goals in life are similar.

- You enjoy doing participating in activities together.

- You enjoy cooking and/or eating together.

- Both of you manage conflicts in a constructive manner.

- You know how to resolve a disagreement between the two of you.

- You have mutual respect for one another.

- You forgive and accept the shortcomings of the other.

- You are satisfied with the manner and frequency of your sexual relations.

- You deeply care for each other.

- You agree about how you are going to raise your children.

- You agree about how you are going to manage your finances.

Take note that this checklist is not all-inclusive in terms of which areas emotional intelligence can make a significant impact on. What you should learn from this is the idea that emotionally intelligent people are better at managing their emotions and their partner's as well.

Here are the other key elements of emotional intelligence that contribute to the success of your relationships:

- Optimism

  Experts on intimate relationships generally agree that an optimistic disposition has the highest correlation with marital satisfaction. As obvious as it may sound, people still overlook the principle that happy people have satisfying relationships with their partners. This is likely because of the possibility that the person becomes happy because he or she is in a positive relationship. Studies suggest, however, that happiness and optimism come first before one can have a fulfilling relationship.

When faced with troubles in their relationship, optimistic individuals try to make the best out of what they have. This means that even if the marriage or relationship is less than perfect, their ability to keep going on allows them to forge ahead despite all the challenges that they are facing at the moment and those that are coming their way.

Optimistic people are also better at handling the stresses of day-to-day living compared to their pessimistic counterparts. Their happiness and motivation tend to rub off on those closest to them—a transfer that causes their positivity to continually spread from one person to another.

- Self-Confidence

  People who are assured of their competence and worth are remarkably resilient when it comes to taking criticisms from others. Doubts and insecurities have little to no place in their minds and hearts, thereby giving them enough boost to communicate with their partner rather than simply keep their feelings of disappointment and resent all to themselves.

- Self-Improvement

  If one or both members of a couple are believers of continual improvement, then their relationship is likely going to be successful in the end. Even if it were just one person pushing the other at the start, this desire to become the best versions of themselves would likely be adopted by the other person, if at least one of them were keen on trying to achieve this no matter what.

- Realism

  Marriages that are grounded to reality tend to be more successful than those that are based on high and unreasonable expectations. Asking for too much from your partner, and feeling disappointed when faced with the reality of the situation are some of the early indicators that the relationship might gradually become toxic and unfulfilling.

To rate how well your relationship is in terms of the emotional bond between you and your partner, follow these steps on how to personally assess your satisfaction with the current state of your relationship:

Step #1: Using a scale of 1 to 5, rate your personal feelings about your relationship—with "1" indicating very low happiness, and "5" representing very happy feelings. Write down your rating on your notebook or journal.

Step #2: List down your favorite aspects of your relationship.

Step #3: List down the things you want to change in your relationship.

Step #4: Rate how motivated you are on making these changes in your relationship. Use the following scale from 1 to 5:

- "1" – "I am not motivated at all to change anything in my relationship."

- "2" – "I am slightly motivated to change some things in my relationship."

- "3" – "I am moderately motivated to change some things in my relationship."

- "4" – "I am highly motivated to change a lot of things in my relationship."

- "5" – I am desperate and more than willing to change anything in my relationship to make me and my partner happier."

If you have rated yourself with at least 3 or above in the first step, your relationship is in a good state, and you are ready to make good into better. Any rating below "3" indicates that you and your partner need to address the issues that may be ruining your happiness with one another. Rating yourself with "5" means that you might want to consider seeking the help of a professional who can help mend your relationship. This is particularly urgent if you cannot think of anything to write on step 2 of the process.

Now, consider the quantity and the degree of how much you want to make changes in your relationship. Rating yourself from "1" to "3" is acceptable since even happy couples have some things to improve upon in their respective relationships. However, if you have rated anything higher than "3", then you might want to consider getting the help of a professional to guide you and your partner on how you can resolve your issues with one another.

Keep in mind the things you have listed down in step 3. Use that information as a reference when you talk about your issues with your partner. Before inviting someone else into your relationship, try and check if you could somehow reach an agreement with your partner in terms of their willingness to accept and make the changes that either of you wants to carry out for the betterment of your relationship.

Emotions and Relationships

A relationship cannot be defined by a single emotion. Saying that discounts the complexities of your partner's and your feelings for one another. It is perfectly normal to have both positive and negative feelings towards your partner. You might have enjoyed having dinner together, but feel annoyed when your partner left the kitchen in a messy state.

Emotions play a vital role in relationships. Depending on how well adjusted you and your partner are, emotions can support the success and longevity of your relationship, or they can also drive a wedge between the two of you.

- Growing Together

  According to experts, emotions can help the relationship grow in two ways:

  - If you were in control of your emotions, you would be able to focus more on strengthening the bond between you and your partner.

  - If you can manage the emotions of your partner, he or she would not be distracted by the nitty-gritty of your everyday life as a couple, thereby letting him or her focus more on the important things that would improve your relationship.

  Being able to self-regulate your emotions is an essential component of successful relationships. When you can maintain a sense of happiness, you would enjoy and be more fulfilled about being in a relationship with another person. You would also be able to withstand tough times together as a team. In this case, your happiness serves as a protective buffer against other unpleasant and destructive emotions that you might have when faced with the challenges of being a couple.

  Managing another person's emotions—if they are not capable of doing it himself or herself—can be quite hard. However, if you truly value your relationship with them, it is worth all the time and effort that you would have to expend to make things work between the two of you.

There is no universal method that could guarantee a stronger bond between people who are in a relationship. Fortunately, experts on marital satisfaction, through years of research and case studies, have gained valuable insights that could lead couples to find the right answer for them. Essentially, their findings suggest that you can tell if your relationship is functioning well by examining the number of positive interactions between you and your partner.

To illustrate their point, imagine your relationship as a bank account. The more positivity your deposit into it, the higher the balance would be. On the other hand, if you interact negatively with your partner, that balance would decrease because you are withdrawing positivity from your relationship. Therefore, it is best to stockpile positivity so that you can be secured even during tough times. As an added bonus, much like money left in your bank account, accumulated positivity also gains interest over time.

In summation, doing good deeds for your partner is similar to why you save up money in the bank. The more you deposit, the more secure you are in the future. As you continue to do so, you would be able to improve your relationship and foster trust with one another.

- Growing Apart

A survey among couples indicates that issues that bring down a relationship happens when one or both partners start to lose interest and take the other for granted. The spark and heat present at the start of the relationship seem to be going away, sometimes without being noticed by the couple until it is too late. To help you assess if your relationship is going down the drain, here is a list of the common signs that you and your partner are growing apart:

- You have stopped greeting or welcoming each other when one of you arrives or comes back home.

- You do not talk about how each of your days has gone by anymore.

- You rarely check in with the other to see how they are feeling, physically, mentally, or emotionally.

- You have stopped engaging in activities that you used to do together.

- Your sexual relationships have become less frequent and/or less satisfying.

- Being together only seems to tire you out.

Agreeing to more than two of the statements given above indicates that you need to have a long, serious discussion with your partner. Check whether you still feel the same way about each other. If you are not certain on how you would proceed with this, try opening up with a simple talk about a recent book you have read about relationships. Share what you have read here, and see if their reaction would be similar to yours. From there, you can bring up a discussion about the current state of your relationship. The best outcome you could hope for is a commitment from both of you to work hard on improving your relationship.

For some people, sustaining a good and healthy relationship is a tough feat to achieve. Being considerate and attuned with one's partner does not come naturally for everyone. There is also the fact that there are certain times when life gets too overwhelming that you do not have a choice but to push away some things to the sidelines. It is unfortunate though that this usually includes one's partner in life.

Those who possess the traits and abilities associated with high emotional intelligence, such as optimism, self-regulation, and self-improvement, find it easier to maintain their respective relationships. Since these are already part of their natural or learned behaviors, they always seek for ways to keep the relationship going in a positive and healthy direction.

If a person does not want to make an effort to adapt to those traits or learn those skills, he or she would eventually think that they are stuck in a rut. The stress would build-up, and might turn into resentment towards one another. Attempts to compromise would become less frequent and less successful. Without making an effort to improve things in a holistic fashion, the romance between couples could die down, leading usually to the complete breakdown of the relationship.

Managing Your Partner's Emotions

As mentioned earlier, managing another person's emotions can take a lot of work from your end. It is a worthwhile endeavor though since doing so could save or improve your relationship. Learning how to read their emotions better would deepen your understanding of their thought and emotional processes, as well as your understanding of your personal perceptions.

To help you in this process, here are the steps you need to take in order to better understand and effectively enhance the emotional state of your partner.

> Step #1: Determine the prevailing emotions of your partner.
>
> Gaining awareness of your partner's current emotions is an essential first step in managing his or her emotions. This shall give you a baseline that you could go back to later on in order to assess the effectiveness of your efforts. It would also be a good basis for the direction of your plans to address the issues in your relationship.
>
> Information on your partner's emotional state can be attained by:
>
> o Listening carefully to the tone of the voice or manner of speaking of your partner;

- Taking note of his or her facial expressions when talking to you; or

- Paying attention to his or her body language when you are nearby.

After you have gathered your initial set of clues, communicate with them and confirm your observations. Do not simply assume that you are right. You might end up jumping into conclusions that are way off base. Explain to your partner as well that you are doing this because you care about him or her as a person, not just about your relationship. This is an important step to make so that your partner would be able to understand where you are coming from, and so that you would gain their cooperation when you try to manage his or her emotions.

Step #2: Form a plan

Now that you know the emotions of your partner, it is time to put things into order, and figure out where you should start. In general, the emotions of your partner would fall into the following categories of mood:

- Happy

- Sad

- Angry

o Anxious

o Calm

Positive emotions such as happiness and calmness should be maintained, or at the very least, be kept from turning into negative emotions. You can do so by doing things that would put your partner in a good mood, and sticking to topics of discussion that both of you find interesting and enjoyable.

You should also include in your plan on how to deal with sensitive topics that bring forth your partner's negative emotions. If you have to talk about them, it is best to pre-arrange the time and day for this so that both of you would have enough time to prepare yourselves mentally and emotionally.

Step #3: Execute your plan.

When executing your plan, keep in mind that your goal is not to avoid disagreements between you and your partner. What you want to create is an environment wherein you can both be honest, but still calm and respectful to one another. Flare-ups of negative emotions cannot be entirely avoided, especially during the early stages. To deal with this, here are some helpful tips for you:

- Listen first, to what your partner has to say without going on a defensive mode.

- When the conversation is becoming too heated, or when your argument becomes stuck in a loop, call for a time out, and agree to resume your discussion after the both of you have calmed down.

- After having your discussion, reflect on how your partner feels about the topic you have talked about.

- Feel free to ask and confirm with your partner if you understand of his or her points and feelings are correct.

- Do not lash out when your partner attacks you with personal criticisms. Listen carefully, and then reflect upon their validity when you are calm.

- Avoid escalating the situation by any means. If your conversation is turning into an argument, take a breather first to deflate the building negative emotions between the two of you.

- Put forward your suggestions to resolve your issues as a couple only when you have a full understanding of the situation and your feelings.

You might think that these strategies are promoting avoidance instead of the effective resolution of your relationship problems. However, pushing forward even if you are burdened with negative emotions is a counterintuitive approach. According to studies, women need to feel like they are being heard first before they could proceed with thinking of possible solutions. Men, on the other hand, tend to launch themselves directly to strategizing ways that would give those results immediately. A balance between these two different perspectives is necessary in order to arrive at actionable and reasonable resolutions that would save your relationship.

Step #4: Respect your partner's limits.

Managing your partner's emotion is not about achieving complete control over him or her. That is not the answer to keeping your relationship stable and healthy. Everyone has opinions about matters that they feel strongly about. It is perfectly okay to disagree on those things, but you do not have to fight over them.

Achieving a successful relationship means that you have to know which topics to stay away from. By doing so, you would be able to eliminate points of friction between you and your partner. If you have to address it at some point, humor is a good buffer for such situations. You can respectfully and humorously disagree with one another as long as you do not use sarcasm or try to put them down with your words.

Managing Your Emotions While You are in a Relationship

Looking outward can only improve your relationship in certain aspects. For a more holistic approach, you have to apply your own emotional skills in establishing a closer relationship with your partner. By doing so, you would be able to enjoy each other's company once more and overcome challenges in your relationship in a more effective manner.

To come up with a good action plan for yourself, consider the following tips on how you can use your emotional skills in your relationship:

Tip #1: Analyze your own emotions after a fight or disagreement with your partner.

In the heat of the moment, most people cannot control their emotions, making them unable to hold back words that they would later regret. Therefore, whenever you feel that your temper is getting the better of you, pause and take a deep breath. Fight the urge to start a screaming match. Instead, count from one to ten in your mind, and feel yourself regaining control over your emotions.

By paying special attention to your own emotions, you would be able to recognize the sizes of impending outbursts that could only harm your relationship. The sooner you are able to do this, the more likely you would be able to change the direction of the situation.

Tip #2: Learn how to pick your battles.

Disagreements come in all sizes and forms. With your partner, it can be as simple as where you should go out for dinner or something as big as whether or not you are going to have children in the future. Not every argument is worth your time, effort, and relationship. You have to know which ones really matter, and which ones you can let go.

Here are some techniques to help you pick the right one that is worth standing up for:

o   Choose something that is doable. Do not challenge your partner to change his or her behaviors that started since childhood, or urge him or her to lose an unreasonable amount of weight.

o   Choose something that holds significant meaning for both of you.

- Do not go after your partner's personality. Instead, choose something that can be changed even without professional help.

- When you have chosen a behavior, you want your partner to change, set a goal on when you want this to occur.

- To be fair to your partner, be prepared to change your behavior too if need be.

Tip #3: Figure out when to hold your tongue.

Aside from letting trivial matters go, you should also learn when to shut up instead of trying to win every argument you have. You cannot come out at the top always. Sometimes, you have to sit back, stop talking, and listen to your partner, even if you do not agree with what he or she is saying.

After letting your partner talk, take a few moments to absorb and process their points. You think that their words are ugly and unkind, but remember, their rants might have some sort of basis. Think calmly and try to keep things civil between the two of you. Doing so is not an admission of defeat or guilt. You are only trying to be careful about both of your feelings.

In the end, you would see the benefit of keeping a cool head. Most people who have bad tempers tend to be not taken seriously by the people around them. Some are even avoided because of their lack of self-control. You can avoid being one of them by simply holding your tongue and allowing yourself time to consider your partner's words.

Tip #4: Make the most out of your empathic skills.

Feeling and understanding your partner's feelings does not mean that you have to give in to his or her demands, or take responsibility for something you did not do or say. Instead, it means that you are trying to understand your partner's point of view and that you consider their feelings as valid.

Keep in mind though that applying your empathic skills does not automatically solve the problem for you. It helps though by putting you in a more considerate and forgiving position. Adopting this mindset would prevent you from creating another problem on top of the current issue between you and your partner—a common occurrence that hurts further your relationship.

Learning how emotions affect your relationship is essential in ensuring the success of you and your partner in your decision to spend your life together. Even if one or both of you lack certain skills that are associated with emotional intelligence, you can still work on improving your bond with each other. Just remember that both of you must commit yourselves to achieve your relationship goals.

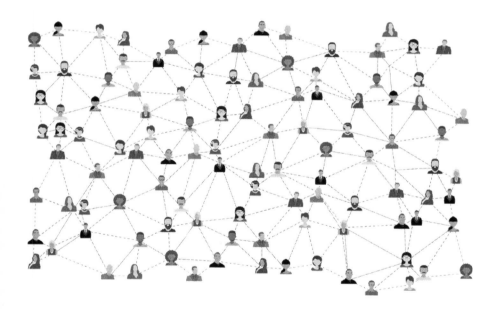

Chapter 18 – Emotional Intelligence and Health

Research shows that there are a direct link between emotional intelligence and health—both physical and mental aspects of one's wellbeing. It is easy to see how emotionally intelligent people are. On the other hand, the effects of emotional intelligence on physical health are by-products of well-regulated emotions and stress level. To better appreciate this relationship, here are the significant effects of emotional intelligence on one's health, as reported by experts.

Mental Health

When left untreated, depression, anxiety, and other forms of mental health issues can have a large impact on the brain. Though nothing could replace professional mental care, working on improving the different aspects of emotional intelligence can help alleviate the effects of these conditions, and even prevent their occurrence altogether. Here are some of the key points revealed by research studies conducted on this:

- A person who understands and can self-regulate his or her emotions feel less lonely or isolated compared to their peers who lack these abilities.

- Being in a strong relationship that is not riddled with arguments and conflicts can lower down one's stress level.

- Practicing mindfulness and adapting a grateful attitude are effective means of calming the mind.

- Laughing and not taking everything, including yourself, too seriously increase the level of appreciation you have towards yourself and those around you.

- Spending quality time with your friends and loved ones can be effective stress relievers.

- Emotionally intelligent individuals are good at communicating their needs to other people.

Physical Health

Majority of the effects of emotional intelligence on health is centered on relieving one's stress. Because of this, serious physical conditions can be prevented, as long as the person also eats a balanced diet, exercises regularly, does not smoke and consume drugs and/or alcohol. The list of the said conditions includes but is not limited to:

- high blood pressure

- heart attack and other heart-related conditions

- stroke

- ulcer

- different types of cancer

Aside from these conditions, stress could also accelerate a person's aging process, as well as contribute to one's infertility or impotence.

The higher the level of emotional intelligence, the better a person's physical and mental health could be. You should not only be kind and caring towards others. Instead, you should also pay attention to your personal wellness. By doing so, you would be able to live a healthier and more holistic life.

Chapter 19 – Emotional Intelligence and Self-Awareness

Emotionally intelligent people are able to identify, describe, and understand their own emotions. They can distinguish one's feelings from another, and they can better predict their reactions towards someone or something. As such, they are in control of the emotional aspects of their personality.

Self-awareness is an important component of emotional intelligence. Do not worry if you believe that you do not possess this trait yet. There are various ways to increase your level of understanding of your own emotions. Explore and discover in this chapter the techniques and strategies that would help you become more aware of your own emotions.

Emotional Vocabulary

Before delving into your attempt to become more self-aware, you need to equip yourself first with the right words to describe your emotional experiences. This is an important aspect of your growth as an emotionally intelligent individual since it would give you the necessary tools to clearly and fully express yourself. This way, others would be able to better understand your perspective and feelings and thus improving your relationship with them.

The English language is rich with adjectives that covers every possible emotional state that humans experience. Positive, negative, and neutral—there is an exact term that would get across the message that you want to convey to those who are around you.

Aside from giving you a more effective means of communicating with others, a wide set of emotional vocabulary would allow you to better understand yourself. Not knowing how to accurately describe how you are feeling could make you feel frustrated. Furthermore, it is hard to address an issue when you cannot even identify what is wrong in the first place.

To help you get started on this, here is an exercise on properly describing the type and intensity of your emotions.

Step #1: Get yourself a journal or notebook for this activity.

Step #2: Review the following terms that are used to label a person's emotional state.

Aggressive	Guilty
Amused	Happy
Angry	Hopeful
Annoyed	Humiliated
Awed	Hurt
Bashful	Jealous
Bored	Lonely
Cheerful	Love-struck
Delighted	Miserable
Depressed	Paranoid
Disappointed	Proud
Disgusted	Regretful
Ecstatic	Sad
Embarrassed	Shocked
Envious	Worried
Excited	
Fearful	
Frustrated	

Step #3: Write down in your notebook the terms that correspond to the emotions that you have had throughout the course of your life.

Step #4: Beside each term, indicate your perception about that particular emotion. To make this simpler, use the following signs:

- "+" – positive emotion

- "-" – negative emotion

- "ø" – neutral emotion

Step #5: Right next to the symbols, rate each emotion from 1 to 10 to determine their respective levels of intensity in terms of how vividly you have an experience that particular emotion. As a reference, use the following anchors for this rating scale:

- "1" – lowest level of intensity

- "5" – average level of intensity

- "10" – highest level of intensity

Step #6: Count the total number of emotions you have written down. Then, break it down to the number of positive, negative, and neutral emotions you have marked earlier. Write down the numbers on your notebook.

Step #7: Get the average ratings for each: positive emotions, and negative emotions. Write down the averages in your notebook.

Step #8: Compare the ratio of positive emotions versus negative emotions. To guide you in your analysis, answer the following questions by looking at the numbers and the emotions in your list:

- o   Have you felt more positive or negative emotions?

- o   Do you feel positive emotions more intensely than negative emotions, or is it the other way around?

- o   Do you think the levels of intensity for each type of emotion have affected how you regard your emotional wellbeing?

Keep in mind that you do not need to label every single emotion that you feel. Stick to the ones that affect you the most, and concentrate on understanding those emotions in relation to other aspects of your life.

Experiencing a wide range of emotions allows people to lead richer and fuller lives. They see things in more than one dimension by putting everything through the lens of their own perspectives. Since they know how to perceive and accurately describe emotions, they are able to interact with others in a more appropriate and considerate manner.

Recognizing and Understanding Your Emotions

Knowing the right words is only the first step of the process. You have to go deep into your mind and discover for yourself the emotions that you are feeling. Getting a sense about how you feel towards a particular person or situation is not enough. You must analyze yourself bit by bit so that you would gain total self-awareness over your emotional side. Here are the different factors that could help you achieve this feat:

- Interpreting the Behaviors of Others

  Have you ever felt like someone's behaviors and feelings were not aligned with what he or she had told you? A new acquaintance might have told you that your story is interesting, but his expression and body gestures tell otherwise. Alternatively, perhaps, a child promises that she has not eaten a single cookie from the jar. However, the way her eyes move and the uncontrollable smirking on her lips seem to tell a different version of the story.

  Since numerous behaviors are automatic responses to certain stimuli or situation, they are good indicators of what a person actually thinks and feels. Similarly, your own behaviors can be picked up by others and give them a clue about your thoughts and emotions.

Given these, you can gradually attain awareness about these aspects of yourself by figuring out the proper way of interpreting the behaviors of other people. You would be able to identify which key behaviors give away valuable information that would otherwise be inaccessible when you only have a superficial interest in these matters.

To help you practice this, here is a simple activity you can while observing other people from a distance. The main goal of this exercise is to show you how to properly structure your observations so that you can gain further insights about yourself later on.

Step #1: Prepare something that you can write on without attracting much attention to yourself.

Step #2: Pretend as if you are an uninterested bystander.

Find a public place where you can blend in with the crowd, and act as if you are merely a bystander. You can be as creative as you want, if you would not stand out from the other people present in that area as well. Common locations that are used for this exercise include hotel lobbies, food courts, parks, and shopping malls.

Some people prefer observing characters in film or television show. However, the obvious drawback of using this method is the lack of emotional authenticity. The emotions being played out are manufactured or drawn out by the script and the commands of another person. For this activity to be more effective, it is better to observe actual people who are exhibiting their natural behaviors and raw emotions.

You should practice this first on your own. When you feel comfortable about observing people from afar, you are ready to proceed with the next step. Some prefer doing this with another person. That is also a good strategy since you can compare your respective observations afterward.

Step #3: Take note of your observations.

On your notebook or note-taking app, create a table with the following headers:

- o   Observed Emotion

- o   Category of Emotion

- o   The intensity of the Emotion

- o   Triggers

- o   Cues

For every situation or scenario that you observe, fill out the table based on your personal assessment. To help you in this step, imagine a scenario wherein you are observing a man and women having coffee together.

- Every time you observe an emotion, write down the label and description in the column for "Observed Emotion."

    For example:

    - Observation A

        ➤ Observed Emotion: "female; happy"

    - Observation B

        ➤ Observed Emotion: "male; worried"

- Next, indicate whether the emotion is positive or negative under the column with the header "Category of Emotion".

    For example:

    - Observation A

        ➤ Observed Emotion: "female; happy"

        ➤ Category of Emotion: "positive"

    - Observation B

        ➤ Observed Emotion: "male; worried"

        ➤ Category of Emotion: "negative"

- In the column for "Intensity of Emotion", rate the intensity of the displayed emotion following a scale of 1 to 10, with 1 being the lowest intensity and 10 being the highest intensity.

  For example:

  - Observation A

    - Observed Emotion: "female; happy"

    - Category of Emotion: "positive"

    - The intensity of Emotion: "6"

  - Observation B

    - Observed Emotion: "male; worried"

    - Category of Emotion: "negative"

    - The intensity of Emotion: "3"

- Try to identify the factors that set off the emotion. Indicate your observations on this in the "Triggers" column.

  - Observation A

    - Observed Emotion: "female; happy"

    - Category of Emotion: "positive"

- The intensity of Emotion: "6"

- Triggers: "grinning slightly, the man said something to her while maintaining eye contact with one another"

- Observation B

  - Observed Emotion: "male; worried"

  - Category of Emotion: "negative"

  - The intensity of Emotion: "3"

  - Triggers: "she dropped her gaze down the cup of coffee in her hand"

  - Cues

- Lastly, in the "Cues" column, indicate the non-verbal cues that led you to believe that the person you are observing is expressing the emotion you have identified. Focus on their facial expressions and body gestures, rather than the words he or she was saying at that given time.

  - Observation A

    - Observed Emotion: "female; happy"

    - Category of Emotion: "positive"

- The intensity of Emotion: "6"

- Triggers: "grinning slightly, the man said something to her while maintaining eye contact with one another"

- Cues: "wide smile, bright eyes, relaxed shoulders"

- Observation B

  - Observed Emotion: "male; worried"

  - Category of Emotion: "negative"

  - The intensity of Emotion: "3"

  - Triggers: "she dropped her gaze down the cup of coffee in her hand"

  - Cues: "furrowed eyebrows, a slight frown on his lips"

Humans are capable of suppressing, denying, or hiding their true feelings. However, no matter how great one is at doing so, one's emotions still manage to subtly reveal themselves. If you can recognize these signals, then you would be able to better understand others, and in the process, gain an understanding of how your mind works as well.

There are also times when your own behaviors confound you. For instance, have you ever avoided a person without any specific or valid reason? Alternatively, perhaps, you have overreacted over a simple statement made by a person who had no ill intentions towards you. In order to make sense of those kinds of situations, you have to look inwards and identify the triggers that caused your seemingly unreasonable behaviors, and figure out how you are going to resolve your personal issues so that you will avoid having any misunderstanding with the people around you.

- Scrutinizing Your Self-Destructive Tendencies

Self-destructive tendencies, such as smoking, overeating, and abusing drugs or alcohol, are revealing of one's emotional and mental health. For example, a study conducted among smokers suggests that his behavior started either out of a need to belong or as a coping mechanism. In the case of the latter, those people believe that smoking makes them look cool or sophisticated. They are also exposed to other smokers, thus making them feel included.

Even if smoking does not necessarily make them feel good, the factors that triggered this behavior would push the person to continue doing this behavior. The need to belong remains, so over time, the behavior would turn into a habit that is hard to shake off. For this very reason, many smokers begin to form this self-destructive tendency during their teenage years.

In most cases, the triggers are emotional. Aside from the need to belong, smokers tend to light up their cigarettes whenever they feel anxious over something they are about to do, or over something that they are going through. Worse, trying to stop smoking could lead to higher levels of anxiety since this would effectively take away their primary means of coping with stressful occasions.

The same principles apply to other people with different self-destructive tendencies. Therefore, if people were able to identify the triggers for this kind of behaviors, they would be able to figure out healthier and more constructive alternative behaviors that would still address their need. However, in most cases, this is easier said than done.

Gaining insight into your self-destructive tendencies is just one-step towards attaining self-awareness. You would begin to understand why you act in a certain way, which is essential in figuring out how you could be a more emotionally intelligent individual. Use these personal insights about yourself to bring yourself closer to your goal of getting better control of your emotions.

- Reading Your Emotions Through the People Around You

There are times when the people around you can recognize your own feelings first before you do. You are focusing on processing the information that you have received without overtly thinking about the reaction that you are expressing at that same moment. Because of this, others are able to become aware of your true feelings even if you want to hide them away from them.

To gain self-awareness of your emotions, it is perfectly all right to seek the inputs of the people around you. Get their feedback and compare them with your own insights about yourself. More often than not, they would be able to tell you something that you have missed out since you are only looking at things from your own perspective.

An emotionally intelligent individual has a high level of self-awareness, especially over his or her habits and attitude towards another person or situation. As such, they are able to understand matters in more than one dimension, thus giving them the ability to come with more sound conclusions and more appropriate action plans.

Achieving self-awareness is not only an introspective activity that you have to do on your own. How you regard others and how others see you reflect your true self as well. Therefore, you should reflect on these aspects of yourself in order to gain a holistic understanding of yourself as an emotional being.

Conclusion

I would like to thank you and congratulate you for transiting my lines from start to finish.

I hope this book was able to help you discover the true meaning of empathy and emotional intelligence, and how to apply them into your day-to-day life.

The next step is to measure your current level of empathy and emotional intelligence. There are various tests that you can take to ascertain where you stand on the spectrum. By doing so, you would be able to form a better plan on how you could improve your empathic and emotional skills. Highlight the areas that need improvement so that the changes you will make on yourself would have a significant impact on your effectiveness and capability as a social and emotional being.

I wish you the best of luck!

Printed in Great Britain
by Amazon

37668667R00097